HUMAN ENGINEERING

HUMAN ENGINEERING

by Lord Robens

Jonathan Cape Thirty Bedford Square London

First published June 1970
Reprinted June 1970
© 1970 by Lord Robens

Jonathan Cape Ltd, 30 Bedford Square, London, wc1

sbn 224 61837 7

Printed and bound in Great Britain
by Butler & Tanner Ltd, Frome and London

Contents

Foreword

It is natural and inevitable that each generation will expect and demand a better life than the last. What constitutes a better life lies in the heart and being of the individual, but for the mass it is represented in growing affluence and a higher standard of living.

This is not just reflected in the demand for increased money incomes to enable the recipient to enjoy the newer features of a modern society: motor cars, holidays abroad, television sets, refrigerators, washing machines, dishwashers, modern homes, modern furniture and wall-to-wall carpets. It also expresses itself in the requirement for increased leisure by shorter hours of labour and longer holidays with pay. The aspiration for a better life leads to demands for substantially improved welfare and medical services, and for modern hospitals built in the second half of the twentieth century. It brings demands for a better educational system beginning with the primary schools, a higher school-leaving age, more universities and substantially improved financial grants for students. It leads to the call to sweep away the last vestiges of the industrial slums that survive as a monument to the Industrial Revolution, to tear down the old towns and build anew, to provide more and better amenities, more concert halls and places for community enjoyment. There are demands to eradicate the pollution of the air, to clean up the rivers and the seas around the populated coasts, and to clear up the thousands of acres of blighted areas of dereliction left by the ravages of industry on its way by.

All these things and a thousand more each generation will pursue as desirable aims. The urge to accomplish these objectives will be constant and there is much impatience with the slowness at which these hopes and aspirations are satisfied.

Every single one of these excellent objectives which people ardently seek to achieve is technically possible. What we need is the national prosperity to pay for it.

It is no use asking Government to provide the wherewithal. Government can only raise money from the people in direct and indirect taxation, and this total sum is limited by the economic growth of the nation.

Economic growth is dictated for an industrial country like the United Kingdom by the growth of world trade and the share of world trade that it can capture by trading competitively. Unfortunately our share of world trade is falling: from 20 per cent in 1955 to 13 per cent today. Why? Because we are pricing ourselves out of the market: we are not competitive.

The blunt truth is that in the ten years from 1953 to 1964 according to an E.E.C. report,* unit costs of production in Britain rose faster than those of our competitors. The increase in labour productivity in the United Kingdom was far lower than in Belgium, Austria, Norway, West Germany, Sweden, Italy, France and the Netherlands. Not something to be very proud about. It was this failure basically that led to the financial crisis and devaluation of the pound in 1967. We could not pay our way because we could not sell enough abroad to pay our bills.

What Britain needs today above all else is industrial efficiency. We cannot survive with an economy running at half capacity. If the people of Britain want superlatively high standards of living; if they want to reach the new horizons; if they really want gracious living and a bright and happier future for them-

* *Economic Survey of Europe in 1965*, Part 2.

selves, their children and the generations to come; and if Britain is to be a dominant influence in the world and its affairs —then the ways and means must be found to exploit to the full the vast potential of the manpower of this country, the native genius and natural initiative, by skilled human engineering. If we could succeed in maximizing the skill and ingenuity of our people, identify and then eliminate all the obstacles to the rapid growth of productivity, then the hopes and aspirations of our nation could be achieved. We could build the New Jerusalem and out of our increased prosperity provide finance for the development of the underdeveloped areas which house over half of the population of the world—a part which lives at or below the poverty line, a smouldering menace to peace and prosperity everywhere else and a lasting reproach to Western civilization. Apart from all other arguments, there is a strong element of self-interest in this: unless Britain and the rest of the more wealthy nations of the world find the means to prime the economic pump of these underdeveloped countries, the advance of those with present prosperity will come to a halt against a barrier of poverty.

It is well within the power and capacity of this country to succeed in this task. Our finest asset, the quality of our people, is largely wasted by under-utilization. Unless ways and means are found substantially to increase the productivity of people at work, then there is simply no hope of achieving the increase in economic growth, without which the full achievement of the nation's ambitions cannot be realized.

Productivity in this country can be raised to much greater heights than most people realize or are prepared to admit. There is no real reason why it should not equal that of the United States, where with more horsepower at the elbow of the worker and with improved management techniques productivity per worker and, as a consequence, the standard of living is higher than anywhere else in the world.

The U.S.A. has scarcely 6 per cent of the world population,

9

and barely 7 per cent of the land and natural resources, yet produces one-third of the world's goods and services. It produces one-quarter of the world's steel, one-third of the world's oil supplies and one-third of the world's electrical energy. It produces almost half of the world's automobiles, more than half of the world's telephones and refrigerators. Three and a half million people go to college every year out of a population of nearly 200 million: more than three times the total of all Western Europe with a population of 340 million people.

Just before the turn of the century the productivity and standard of living of the American industrial worker was roughly the same as his contemporary in Britain. In the period since then, the American industrial worker has increased his productivity four times, compared with twice for his British counterpart.

If we had a productivity equal to that of the United States, our recurrent balance of payments deficit would disappear. Standards of living would be materially improved and our economic problems would be over.

The American worker does not work longer hours, and his higher productivity cannot be attributed to any innately superior intelligence; nor is it based on any techniques that are not well known. The Americans lose more days in labour disputes pro rata to their working population than we do. So how is it done?

Simply by far better utilization of labour than we have been able to effect in this country.

With the right kind of human engineering from shop floor to boardroom and everything in between, we too could be prosperous once again. There is no magic about this: the secret is simply the most efficient use of our labour force, together with enlightened and efficient management.

There is a mistaken idea that somehow or other good industrial relations can be secured by law. This of course is not so.

Law can only enforce the rules. But the rules have to be agreed between unions and management: they cannot be unilaterally enforced. That up-to-date legislation needs to be enacted to meet the conditions of modern times there can be no doubt. At best, however, the law-makers can only lay down the guidelines of good behaviour. Good industrial relations cannot be measured solely by the number of strikes, official or unofficial. They are based on willingness to co-operate, particularly in the introduction of new techniques, and readiness to help solve modern commercial and production problems. This entails a completely new approach both by management and workpeople, with the emphasis upon managerial attitudes: for that is where power and authority and leadership lies.

We are pretty good at engineering in this country. Indeed this is where it all started. But we have failed in our human engineering: a term I shall use to describe all those various ways in which modern techniques and philosophies of human relations in industry are utilized to ensure on the one hand a sense of fulfilment to the individual at work and on the other the maximum contribution by the individual to industry.

There is no single way in which we can say we have failed, because management-labour relations have many facets. All these sides of the problem must be examined to discover where weaknesses exist so that corrective action can be taken. This book deals with the main aspects of human engineering in industry. It brings together those elements of human engineering so often neglected in part or in whole. Negotiating wages and conditions is only part of the subject: a sensitive and important part it is true, but nevertheless still only one part of a complex that makes up human industrial society. There is no blueprint which will speedily and effectively solve the many vexed problems of man at his work, but there can be no doubt that where skill and care have been taken to solve these problems, great success has resulted. But it has to be emphasized time and time again that the same kind of forethought and precision is required in dealing with every aspect of human engineering as is put into the fine engineering for the Space Programme. The results can and will be just as spectacular.

1 Bricks Without Straw

We cannot make bricks without straw, cried the people of Israel; but Pharaoh insisted that the amount of bricks to be made should not be lessened merely because the supplies of raw material had been withheld. Instead he ordered that the brick-makers should go out and gather straw for themselves. This made the task of brick-making harder, but bricks continued to be made as the stubble in the fields was gathered and brought to the brick-makers.

On the face of it, one would assume that countries which already possessed the raw materials for manufacture would become wealthy and powerful while those without an abundance of raw materials would remain comparatively poor and life there extremely hard.

But the story of Britain is just the reverse. Looking back over the last three centuries of British history one sees a land with comparatively few natural resources rise to great prosperity and wielding great power and influence throughout the world.

Who, at the beginning of the seventeenth century, would have predicted that the first great industrial power would be Great Britain, a predominantly agricultural country with few natural resources and with no apparent advantages over the great nations of the time, France and Spain? Other countries had far greater resources in terms of fuel and other raw materials which were to be vital in the early years of industrialization.

13

Why then was it Great Britain and not, say, China or Russia which sparked off the Industrial Revolution? The answer is that while a supply of the appropriate raw materials is an essential precondition for industrial take-off, they lie dormant unless people have a will and a way to exploit them. Britain was an industrial pioneer only through the skill and perseverance of her manpower, the inventiveness and genius of her engineers, and the zest and common sense of her management. It was the quality of our people alone which interrupted the even procession of history and broke through to fashion an entirely new form of society.

Suitable raw materials are an enormous asset, but the potential of a country can lie undiscovered and unexploited unless the inhabitants have the energy and the ability to turn the potential into something real. It was the human element in Britain that was the prime mover in our industrial development. It is upon the same human element that our future prosperity will rest.

The will to set out along the road to industrial maturity arose from the attitudes and outlook of later seventeenth- and eighteenth-century Britain. These attitudes may have been born in the Dissenting and Nonconformist chapels of Britain, but the ideas and notions spread throughout almost every section of the community. These were the beliefs that the successful are the elect of God, that independence of mind and action are primary virtues and that thrift and sobriety are the hallmarks of the righteous man.

If this impelled the will, the way was laid by scientific and technological invention, starting with the spirit of inquiry and innovation developed by the Royal Society and spreading in the eighteenth century to the entrepreneurs and practical men of the manufacturing areas.

Some of the most successful early mill-owners uniquely combined the roles of businessman and inventor. Such a man was Richard Arkwright. Born in Bolton in 1732, the thirteenth child of poor parents, he started life as a barber, but gave this up at thirty-five in order to devote himself to the invention and perfection of a spinning frame powered by water. Subsequently he moved to Nottingham where he built his first spinning mill. Three years later, in partnership with and financed by two stocking manufacturers, he built a larger factory at Cornford in Derbyshire. He went on to build more mills in Derbyshire and Lancashire and helped to build the mills at New Lanark. He amassed a fair fortune, and built Wiberley Castle and Cornford Church. He died in the former and was buried in the latter in 1792.

Thus Richard Arkwright, starting life as a barber, became an inventor more than halfway through his life, then became the richest cotton-spinner in England with a fortune of half a million pounds at the end of his days. Carlyle* later said of Arkwright:

> What a historical phenomenon is that bag-cheeked, pot-bellied Lancashire man, much enduring, much inventing barber.

Carlyle could have said this about many of the early businessmen; what historical phenomena they were! However, if we are to turn once again to the development of human resources we should be looking not for the old attributes that served us well, but for a new range of qualities. Modern industrial organization probably could not digest a new Arkwright. If such a man were recruited as a workman he would quickly be picked out as a trouble-maker; if he joined as a management trainee he would be even more rapidly identified as someone who 'won't fit in'. So we should be shaping our human resources in new forms to suit the modern industrial situation.

Whilst we can be considered fortunate to have had the right conjunction of social attitudes amongst the early entrepreneurs to give us a head start in the race, it is Britain's lasting

* 'Essay on Chartism', *Critical and Miscellaneous Essays*, Vol. 3 (Chapman & Hall, 1869).

misfortune that this conjunction should have taken place in a land only half stocked with the necessary raw materials for industry. Our assets were (and still are) human ones and our physical assets, never good, are growing less and less relevant. In human beings we are strong but in natural resources we are weak. We are still today a nation whose only real asset is the quality of our people.

Our lack of natural resources determined that if we were to be a major industrial nation we must also be a major trading nation. To pay for the raw materials of manufacture we have always had to sell abroad the products of industry. The industrial nations which have followed us have not had this disadvantage. America, Russia and several European countries have been blessed with many of the natural advantages we have lacked, and therefore they have not had the problems which arise from being a trader.

Our position as a trading nation may have its disadvantages from our point of view, but at the same time it had enormous advantages for the underdeveloped world. We needed the raw materials in great quantities and varieties and people were engaged in the underdeveloped world to provide the things that were needed for Britain's factories. They became 'primary producers'. Income was generated, manufactured goods were imported to supply new needs and the foundation of future development of those countries was laid. If Britain had possessed within her own shores all the raw materials she needed, then the primary producing nations would have remained underdeveloped for many years. This was an accidental outcome of Britain's industrialization, and to most historians the benefits to the underdeveloped countries have been less apparent than the advantages Britain derived from cheap raw materials. But there can be no doubt that to her own ultimate disadvantage Britain showed the way of industrial development to many countries which have now become her rivals.

Whatever its ultimate advantages to the world, our need to

be a trading nation as well as an industrial nation has left Britain with serious handicaps. It was not difficult to sell abroad the vast quantities of manufactured goods necessary to sustain a rapidly expanding population when we had the field to ourselves. But the technological surge in Britain rapidly triggered off a chain reaction in the countries of Europe and North America which already enjoyed several advantages. First, they often possessed all the raw materials that were needed at that time. Secondly, they were able to learn by our mistakes and copy only the best of our techniques.

Then there was also a third and compelling urge. It became increasingly clear to the countries producing primary products that they would never be affluent if they remained solely suppliers of raw material. Power and rapidly rising standards of living belonged to those nations who turned primary products into consumer and capital goods: it was in the fields of manufacture that the rich rewards lay. One by one developing nations learned this lesson, and indeed were taught to do so by the manufacturers of machines, whose whole interest lay in selling their wares.

Perhaps the cotton industry is the most graphic example of this aspect of change, the cotton industry which is both the starting-point and the prime example of the development of Britain as an industrial power. Cotton has been described as the thread that runs through the Industrial Revolution. Industrial Britain was born in Lancashire's damp valleys and the life cycle of the nation has in many aspects been the life cycle of cotton writ large. It is typical in a way that it should be cotton, an imported commodity, transported many thousands of miles, that began it all.

The economic individualism of the late eighteenth and nineteenth century found its most complete expression in the Lancashire cotton trade. Right from the very start it was the quality of people which counted for most in the take-off of the Lancashire cotton industry. True, port facilities and power supplies were freely available but the Lancashire cotton industry was the work of man rather than nature.

The fashion for East Indian cottons introduced in the seventeenth century provided Lancashire with the opportunity. The early inventors, and in particular the inventor entrepreneurs such as Richard Arkwright, provided the means by which the new fashions could be exploited.

By 1800 cotton-spinning had to a large extent become a factory trade, although it was not until after 1815 that steam-power could be said to have displaced water-power. In the weaving branch the change came later: a power loom capable of competing with the hand loom was not placed on the market until 1822. After 1830 the number of hand looms declined and weaving passed into the mills, but the hand loom weaver was not displaced until 1860.

During the latter half of the nineteenth century there were small-scale improvements but no fundamental changes in techniques. Further expansion in the second half of the nineteenth century could only have come through the multiplication of known techniques. Between 1885 and the First World War spindlage rose nearly 44 per cent to nearly 60 million spindles in 1914. Looms rose 47 per cent in the same period to 805,000 in 1914.

Cotton quickly overtook our traditional export, wool. In 1913, at the end of the era in which Britain was the pre-eminent industrial nation, cotton accounted for a quarter of all British exports and three-quarters of the total output of the industry went overseas.

For the spinning and weaving towns of Lancashire this was the height of their power and prosperity. But the downward slope from the pinnacle was made steeper and harsher by the disruption and distortion of the First World War.

Bolton, for example, after a century of rapid growth was at its population peak of 180,000. Since 1918 the downward trend in population has continued almost to the present day. Even as late as the period from 1957 to 1961, forty-eight cotton mills in Bolton were closed.

There was a brief artificial boom for a few years after the First World War, but very quickly the new situation made itself felt in the cotton towns of Lancashire. Demand at home was fairly well maintained throughout the inter-war period and the declining output was entirely the result of the collapse of the overseas trade: while Britain was in decline the output of cotton goods in the rest of the world continued to rise. Home production grew up in countries previously supplied by Britain, especially in the underdeveloped world. Countries such as India, where cotton was indigenous, began to exploit their own potential. Cotton manufacture was a relatively simple form of production and in many countries there was already a tradition of spinning and weaving on a craft basis. In the absence of any natural advantages or the development of further technical innovations, Lancashire was bound to suffer.

At the same time, other developing industrial nations were expanding production and competing for the world markets. By 1934, after having led the field for two centuries, Britain was surpassed by Japan as the largest supplier of cotton goods in the world.

When economic measures, such as the Import Duties Act of 1932, the Ottawa Agreement and the Colonial Quota System had failed to halt the decline, more direct steps were taken through the Redundant Spindle Act of 1936 and the establishment of the Cotton Industry Board under the Enabling Act of 1939. Nothing, however, could alter the fact that the structure of world trade and our position in the world economic system had changed beyond recognition.

The trials of the cotton industry are important to the argument of this book because they are a frightening indication of how British industry could evolve if we should fail to develop the potential of this country in the right way and fail to do it soon enough.

This is the situation in Britain today. On the debit side Britain has a backlog of superseded techniques because it was the first great industrialized country, and now suffers a continual struggle to maintain international solvency, among other reasons, because of the necessity for huge imports of the raw materials for feedstocks for industry. On the credit side we have the British people, uniquely experienced in the rhythm of industrial life. My proposition is that Britain can show a profit on the balance between these two, by concentrating on developing the things that are best in her. It was the human resources that gave Britain its early lead and we should now seek to capitalize on that asset to the full. This is the objective of what I have called human engineering.

Quite rightly we have accepted full employment as a cardinal principle of economic life. At the same time, it has meant that we have lost industrial discipline in this country. The threat of the sack was a crude, inhumane instrument, but we have so far failed as a nation to find a substitute. Attitudes on both sides of industry today continue to result in the misapplication of manpower. Many of us in the 1930s believed that once there was full employment, adequate provision for those who through sickness or misfortune could not earn their own living, an educational system such that every man could receive the schooling for which he was most fitted, and real equality of opportunity, then in an atmosphere of social justice men would work together vigorously, harmoniously and efficiently. Britain would then, it was thought, develop in an orderly and efficient manner to the benefit of everyone. Many people like myself who fought in the trade union and Labour movement for all these things are today sometimes dismayed by the course that British people have chosen for themselves.

Nevertheless, I still believe that the potential is there to be realized if only individual and collective talents can be exploited to the full. But this will not happen until we turn our attention to what Robert Owen called our 'living machines'.

In human relations, in training, in management development, in communication and in consultation, nothing short of a revolution is needed in order to make the fullest use of this human potential. In recent years we have seen some tragic examples of wrong-headed industrial relations which demonstrate too clearly the need for a complete change in attitudes. For example, in some industries managers have adopted the philosophy that trouble can be bought off. Instead of seeking out the real cause of disputes their reaction to problems has been to reach for their cheque-books when they should have been down on the factory floor finding out what are the real causes of trouble.

Until human relations are harmonized, human capabilities will be smothered in an atmosphere of conflict and unease. Men must be trained in new and relevant skills to keep up with changing technology. As skills become more specialized, adult education will have to take on a new role in the widening of men's vision. In management development we must recognize that it is management ultimately who shape the character and set the purpose of our enterprises; management that at the highest level can see the totality of policy decisions for five and ten years ahead, using all the modern techniques of market research, operational research and the like, ensuring that the computer is fed with the right material so that it spews out the right answers from the indigestible mass of basic figures that only the human mind can prepare.

As industrial firms become larger, by growth and merger, the need for good communications becomes even more urgent. The essence of industrial democracy is the right of every man to be considered and for no man's opinions to be suppressed, and this should be the aim in joint consultation.

The much vaster industrial, manufacturing and service units require a completely different type of management from the old. We shall need new methods of administration that eschew the long paper-chase that clutters up and clogs the machinery:

administration that is streamlined, efficient and effective, that understands and practises the art and skill of delegation and prevents the creation of alibis for work badly done.

Accountability will need to acquire a new meaning in those corporations, ever growing in size, with their self-perpetuating managements, where the shareholders' writ is becoming smaller and smaller and diminishing in most cases to a well-organized annual meeting with tea and buns and a free sample of the product thrown in.

All these topics should receive the fullest attention. We could develop the finest machines, embodying the latest technology, and yet unless we get our human relations right all the money we spend on research and development will come to nought.

Many of our present economic difficulties arise from our failure in the past to develop the potential of human resources. We have sacrificed these resources through neglect. When we look at the economic history of the present half-century there are numerous examples of policies which disregard the importance of people.

Britain's present economic problems are not solely the outcome of the post-war years. The deficit in the visible trade balance has been with us ever since the 1920s but has been masked by invisible earnings from shipping, insurance, banking earnings on overseas investments, etc. Today it is essential to get much nearer to a visible trade balance because the present invisible earnings are largely swallowed up by Government expenditure overseas and the need for the repayment of international loans.

We are not therefore faced with a brand new economic problem. Two wars in a generation have certainly accelerated a situation that was, however, already arising. One can see this if the period since 1914 is examined against the background of the international position.

Until 1914 the United Kingdom, France and Germany were the only important net creditors on international capital

22

account, and until then international transactions went fairly smoothly. Britain's widespread trading empire made London a useful and dependable centre for international transactions. The First World War interrupted the steady progress of settling and renewing debts. The movement of commodities was diverted from traditional channels as the world took up station in two opposing camps. Factories turned from the production of export goods to weapons of war. In 1913 a large proportion of what the U.K. produced went overseas. By 1918 that proportion had halved.

The warring nations naively assumed that trade was only temporarily suspended. They imagined that after hostilities were over, trade with the rest of the world would be resumed unchanged. But while Europe was locked in combat, the other nations of the world had turned elsewhere for their goods. Some had set up factories of their own and others turned aside to trade with nations not so heavily engaged in the war.

By the time the war had ended, many nations had bled themselves white but even then blood-letting still went on in Poland, Turkey and Russia. Totally unrealistic reparations were demanded by the victorious powers. In 1921 the Reparations Commission demanded £6,500 million from Germany, which was totally incapable of paying.

Industry and transport were utterly disorganized. The relative values of different currencies varied wildly in a short space of time and this uncertainty choked a lot of trade to death. Debtor nations became creditors. Some nations had sold off their vast investments overseas; the U.K.'s foreign investments for example were reduced by 25 per cent. In 1924 the Dawes plan tried to put war reparations on a sounder footing.

Between the wars production at home was stagnant or declining. Between 1921 and 1932 the gross national product fell by over 20 per cent from £5,128 millions to £4,024 millions.

Externally the position was even more serious. Between 1920

and 1966 Britain imported £107,000 millions worth of goods and during the same period exported £78,000 million, leaving a trade gap of £29,000 million. This is equivalent to the entire national product in 1965. Between 1920 and 1929 invisible exports provided a fairly healthy external trade balance. From 1930 onwards invisible exports have not been sufficient to make up the balance on import/export gap.

The chaotic state of international payments led to serious mistakes in home policy. These mistakes allowed a grave neglect of human potential. It is worthwhile examining one of these policy decisions in more detail.

By the early 1920s Britain had talked herself into a return to the Gold Standard. This in itself was part of the delusion of the era that wars are no more than a brief and unpleasant hiatus in the steady progress of history. By tying the British pound to a given weight of gold the politicians, bankers and economists concerned thought that they could whistle back the noble past into a new existence — a sort of transmigration of our economic soul. They considered too that the Gold Standard was the emblem of Britain's greatness and national pride and that the return to gold would conjure up past glory.

By April 1925 Winston Churchill was able to proclaim the return to gold at its pre-war parity. Yet some of the most gifted men of the age voiced their opposition. John Maynard Keynes challenged both the theory and the practice of a return to gold. He pointed out the folly in practice of a return to the pre-war parity, which meant that the pound would be over-valued to the extent of about 10 per cent. British price levels were too high to sustain the pre-war rate. A given quantity of gold in 1925 could command considerably fewer British goods than it could in 1910. What was really needed was a devaluation of the pound. Britain's competitive position as a trading nation took a serious knock. Imports were cheaper and exports dearer. As our trading position weakened, so we had to maintain high interest rates in order to keep foreign funds in the London banks. Dear money depressed investment. All this made a decisive contribution to the depressed state of British industry from 1925 to 1929 at a time when America, for example, was enjoying a gigantic boom.

Keynes criticized too the whole theory of a gold standard whose workings depended upon automatic responses to changes in gold reserves. Countries refused to act mechanically in the face of gold movements. When London was virtually the sole centre for exchange and credit the system could be operated fairly successfully, but in the post-war situation other rival financial centres had sprung up which made the operation of the system impossible. The international monetary structure had altered beyond recognition, and Britain's attempt to graft on to this new body a part of the old could lead only to disaster.

The period 1925 to 1931, when Britain was saddled with an over-valued currency, is worth looking at because they are the middle years of a period in our history when those in positions of authority failed to recognize the importance of human resources and their vital contribution to the national well-being. The industrial goodwill and co-operation which had been born out of wartime conditions quickly evaporated in a situation in which the men at the top had become enchanted with a dream that the old world could be again called into being by the restoration of gold. Nothing could have been further from the truth. Human potential was wasted on a vast scale by the appalling blight of unemployment. This situation has left an almost permanent scar on industrial relations.

Before the First World War, unemployment averaged 4 per cent to 5 per cent. The high points were 1908 and 1909 when the figure was almost as high as 8 per cent. Yet from 1920 to the Second World War, unemployment fell below 10 per cent only twice.

In 1925 there were 1·3 million unemployed, or 11·3 per cent of the working population. By 1930 this had mounted to 2 million, or 16 per cent. By 1932 there were 2·8 million out of work or 22·1 per cent. Yet since the Second World War, unemployment has never been more than 3 per cent, except for a few months in 1963 when it rose to 3·9 per cent. In all, hundreds of millions of days' work were lost through unemployment between the wars. Most of these days could have been put to good use in preparing Britain for a new industrial advance.

Britain's return to gold was by no means the predominant reason for our economic ills in the inter-war period. On the other hand it illustrates the sort of approach to the nation's economic affairs which ignores our only real asset, human beings, and looks for solutions in fiscal policies.

In the inter-war period, the failure to develop the full potential of our manpower resources was due to neglect — the leaders of the time mindlessly allowed men to find their way to the social scrap-heap. In the 1960s our fault is not so much neglect as misuse.

Now that the kind of poverty we knew in the 'twenties and the 'thirties has gone for the bulk of the population, now that there is a job for most people and reasonable maintenance for those without, with growing affluence and the end to worries about providing the bare essentials, one might have expected a new situation to have arisen. A more affluent society provides the climate in which a new concept of living might have emerged, in which some of the Christian virtues might have become manifest: affluence without greed; advancement based on personal effort and initiative; a move away from lawlessness and crime. But these things have not happened. With growing affluence there is growing selfishness, greed and disregard for others. There is a sickness revealed in the increasing concern with vested interests displayed by almost every section of society.

Crime and drug addiction are the daily meat of the newspapers, and the abuse of the services of the Welfare State has become such a scandal that even those who regarded these benefits as the most sacred of sacred cows are ready to lead them to the slaughter-house.

Even with the Welfare State, full employment, and an educational system which recognizes talent as well as birth, we have still failed to get our human relations right.

A fundamental re-examination of the way in which men work and live together in this country could be the starting-point of a re-awakening of enterprise which is so badly needed to get this country back into the front line of industrial nations. We must look closely at our potential, identify our bad points and seek out our good.

In terms of natural resources, we are in an even poorer position than we were at the beginning of the industrial revolution. No useful new asset has come to light in the last two hundred years, apart from natural gas and the ability to exploit nuclear energy. Although these discoveries are stimulating ones, the benefits will only come through a fairly small contribution to the build-up of energy requirements over the next thirty years. Britain should turn her attention fairly and squarely to the asset which first launched her on the road to an industrial society. This is our living asset: the people of Britain.

The efficient use of manpower in every industry and service, involving the ready acceptance of new techniques, the elimination of industrial disputes, strikes, go-slows and the like, would put this country back into its leading role, produce an affluence undreamed of, and enable us much more generously to relieve poverty in other parts of the world.

The New Jerusalem will not come from chanting slogans or passing resolutions. It can only come by the efficient application of all our human resources to the tasks in hand.

Management and men have much to learn from one another and each must recognize the importance of their respective roles.

The mood of the closing decades of the twentieth century is a restlessness born out of the speed of change, the tempo of which increases year by year. There is therefore no time to lose. Time lost can never be recaptured. Equally, time taken by the forelock could change the British economy out of all recognition.

Today it is quite possible to make bricks without straw. But while we can replace the natural fibres of cotton and wool by man-made fibres from glass and plastics, there is no replacement for the human being. New machines can take the drudgery out of production but additional skills are needed to design and produce them. Fewer and fewer people may be needed actually to produce capital and consumer-goods but more and more people will be required in the back-rooms and for the servicing of the new wealth and extra leisure time.

If a constantly expanding economy is to be secured without undue inflation, the intelligent application of people to the various tasks is all-important. In a modern society technical engineering evolves, but human engineering must be made to happen. There are certain skills and techniques that must be used but, in the main, human engineering is a matter of plain common sense and an attitude of mind. Above all it is a recognition that however humble a job may be, those who have to do it are people, with the same hopes and aspirations as others, the same domestic and financial problems as most, the same human characteristics that all people share in some degree or other, and the same ability both to give and to take offence. A society that recognizes that people matter more than machines, that encourages the best in people, is a society that can make bricks without straw and sell them profitably as well.

There can be no doubt about the ability of the British people to develop new techniques and modern physical engineering, but we shall neglect at our peril the problems that surround the art and skill involved in human engineering.

2 Work and Industry

The theme is a simple one: people count. In politics as in industrial management one must continuously interpret situations in terms of what the potential is for those people who are involved. Every measure and every move, every policy and every project should be a permanent quest to reclaim the sunken areas of man's potential, and exploit the capacity to take advantage to the full of life and its possibilities.

This should be the touchstone of all we do. Three principles are common to virtually every moral and political system: the need to provide for bodily requirements, the need to provide for human fellowship and the need to promote the development of the human mind. Properly managed, the modern industrial economy can certainly provide for man's physical needs and the family remains the chief agency of human fellowship, that is, man's social requirements. But industry, though so effective in providing for the body, frequently does little for the mind. It is this aspect, this need to provide for mental well-being and self-realization, which bothers so many.

The dulling awkwardness of work in our factories and offices is a major obstacle to progress in the great trek towards the development of man as a sophisticated and civilized individual. How can industry be made the vehicle of this achievement rather than a hindrance to it? It is salutary to look back into history and trace step by step what industrialization did to those who crowded the factories and mines and the legacy of that formative period which set the pattern of today's industrial society.

These changes which took place in Britain two hundred years ago were more than an industrial revolution: they were a revolution in human terms as well. This was a period of great human change. At first change was slow, but soon there was built in to our society a motor of renewal and progress which today is still altering men's outlook as rapidly as it is remodelling the shape of their surroundings. From those beginnings of two centuries ago we have gradually learned the trick of change —a change which has had its most profound impact on the lives and livelihood of human beings.

If these industrial changes were a revolution in human terms, it is only right that people over the years should have asked themselves whether the whole process was worthwhile, in particular for the men, women and children in the early days who manned the newfangled machines. This is a debate in which this book cannot take sides. It would, however, be right to say this: it is easy to appreciate the point of view of those who, at the very start of industrialization, despaired of the new manufacturing processes and could see nothing in it but misery for the people. But few would deny that we are today enjoying the pay-off in terms of our standard of living. Those early critics, often sensitive poets and philosophers, contrasted what they saw of life in the new industrial towns with a serene rural husbandry that existed chiefly in their own minds.

Robert Southey, the poet, said:

> ... the new cottages of the [workmen] are ... upon the manufacturing pattern ... naked, and in a row. How is it, said I, that everything which is connected with manufactures presents such features of unqualified deformity? ... Time cannot mellow them; Nature will neither clothe nor conceal them; and they remain always as offensive to the eye as to the mind.

And how right he was: the 'naked cottages' are our present-day squalid slums, which despite valiant efforts of slum clearance still remain with us, a monument to the era of great environmental change. The critics saw that factory conditions, long hours and overcrowding were disastrous to health and happiness. In contrast, the fields and farms they left behind were healthy, happy and carefree.

There was no lack of people to point out the evils of the working environment in the early mines and factories. Unhealthy, unpleasant and dangerous places they were, of that there is no question.

In 1815, Robert Owen wrote:

> The general diffusion of manufactures throughout a country generates a new character in its inhabitants; and as this character is formed upon a principle quite unfavourable to individual or general happiness, it will produce the most lamentable and permanent evils, unless its tendency be counteracted by legislative interference and direction ... This alteration is still in rapid progress, and, ere long, the comparatively happy simplicity of the agricultural peasant will be wholly lost amongst us.

The title of the pamphlet from which this is an extract is worth quoting in full: 'Observations on the Effect of the Manufacturing System with hints for the improvements of those parts of it which are most injurious to health and morals: dedicated most respectfully to the British Legislature'. One is bound to add that if many of us had been alive in those days we might not have addressed our observations quite so respectfully to the British Legislature.

When, later in the century, Charles Dickens drew his portrait of an industrial centre which he christened Coketown in his book *Hard Times*, still little could be found to commend the new towns. In this way an unbending antagonism towards industry and the industrial town persisted well beyond the early days

31

of the first factories and factory towns. The contrast between healthy, peasant Arcadia and dangerous industrial Coketown has lingered in men's minds long after the comparison has grown false.

The early experiences of the Industrial Revolution have struck deep into our philosophy and outlook. Even today there is a strong undercurrent of feeling that industry is somehow a distorting and dangerous influence.

The predominant nineteenth-century philosophy of non-interference by the State ensured that improvements in working conditions could only be brought about after the most profound heart-searching. It was felt, often quite genuinely, that interference in factory conditions was an outrage to workmen's self-esteem. Each man should control his own destiny, and to intervene even to help him would ultimately destroy his ability to handle his own life.

Those early raw days of industrialization brought together a cruel conjunction: the human dislocations caused by rapid industrial changes and the growth of factory towns were harsh enough in themselves; but when these conditions were combined with a philosophy which deplored any measure which could better the human condition then it is not surprising so many should have regretted so strongly the savagery of the early years.

Yet the potential rewards of successful industrialization are boundless. The opportunities of improving the standard and style of life are a justification by themselves for our transformation into an industrial society. Industrial development can provide the means of reducing the tragedy of poverty in the underdeveloped countries of the world. Modern standards of medicine and hygiene can be blamed for the population explosion, but it is only through the inventions and developments of modern science that the poorer nations can be fed, clothed, housed and educated.

Yet work has bothered man long before science and technology were infused into its operations. It has been a major issue from time immemorial.

The Biblical view, in the third chapter of Genesis, is that work as a human activity began when Adam was expelled from the Garden of Eden as a punishment for gross disobedience. At that time the Lord offered very little hope of job satisfaction for the future. 'In the sweat of thy face shalt thou eat thy bread.'

We are now in the mechanized age and much of the sweat has been taken out of human labour. But is work still a punishment? For thousands of years man has objected to work because of the toil it entails. Now much of this toil has gone, or is going, and man is bewildered by the fact that for the majority there is still no satisfaction in work. There have now arisen new ground rules for discontent. Some say all work is boring, that it fails to develop the total man, and is unconnected with the pleasures of life. Whatever the reasons, the symptoms of unrest are there: strikes, low efficiency, bloodymindedness, resentment. The demise of hard, grinding, physical labour has not ushered in the New Jerusalem. Yet engineering and science, agencies which are abolishing the hard grind in work, can also provide enormous interest and stimulation for all.

This is the perplexing paradox. Engineering and science can, on the face of it, reduce human toil and also exercise the mind in new directions. We now have at our disposal powers to control and direct nature. We are uniquely able to create and mould an environment in which human potential can be realized to the full. These are all the opportunities that science applied to industry has created, and yet the discontent of the early days of the Industrial Revolution still stalks in our manufacturing towns today and added to it are new symptoms of unrest, boredom and frustration. The early promise of science has not been fulfilled.

William Cobbett said, 160 years ago:

England has long groaned under a commercial system,

c

which is the most oppressive of all possible systems; and it is, too, a quiet, silent, smothering oppression that it produces, which is more hateful than all others.

Is industrial society still a smothering oppression? Is it still not possible to earn a living in industry and at the same time be at peace with mind and neighbour? Can we make modern technology the servant, not the master, of modern man? Can a new attitude towards work evolve in the atmosphere of modern technology?

The two great citizen armies of the First and Second World Wars provided new experience in personnel selection. Mass conscription meant that every week thousands of men had to be quickly and efficiently tested and assessed for adaptability and training in new skills. This experience has provided a peacetime service too. School leavers and others can now be given vocational guidance based upon well-tried principles. As a result it should now be more and more common for men and women to find themselves in a job for which they are best suited.

Not only this, but we now have an educational system which is approaching equality of opportunity. At the end of the last century the great scientist and visionary Thomas Huxley looked forward to an age when there was an educational ladder from 'the gutter to the university'. One need not take the gutter as a starting-point, but we certainly have the ladder installed. So one would expect more and more square pegs in square holes. But this does not seem to have happened and still work seems to bring little satisfaction.

It is instructive to look at some of the attitudes our forefathers took towards the work that they did. Man has regarded the task of earning his living from different points of view at different times. The predominant attitude of the Greeks was one of disdain. Work was something to be avoided if at all possible. The highest form of human activity was calm contemplation, unsullied by the day-to-day cares of the world. In an ideal society, philosophers would be kings and kings would be philosophers. They took, oddly enough, a rather Biblical view. They felt keenly that work was almost a punishment—like the curse God put on Adam as he was 'sent down' from the Garden of Eden. This particular viewpoint, one feels bound to add, could only be sustained amongst the privileged minority in a slave society.

The medieval ideal was that each man should find his ultimate self-fulfilment through working with his hands and his mind in the creative unison of real craftsmanship. The handicraft technology of the age allowed a painstaking skill to be employed throughout the manufacturing process, from handling the raw materials to the final touches of a finished article.

This ideal could only survive in the era before the application of power to machines splintered and scattered the industrial process into numerous repetitive processes. The opportunity of seeing the process of manufacture in the round from beginning to end was destroyed. These changes in the technique of production and the profile of work did not prevent nineteenth-century thinkers like Ruskin, Morris and Tolstoy from trying to transplant the beguiling craftsman ideal into a mechanized age. Again in the twentieth century this tempting and satisfying work philosophy is acted out in a million homes every week-end, when the husband turns to a hobby and re-enacts the medieval craftsman's ideal in digging his garden, building a cupboard or re-decorating his home.

The Nonconformist attitude was embodied in the slogan 'Man's self-love is God's Providence', and one did not have to be a chapel-going Nonconformist to believe in this theory. It encompassed the belief that hard work and success in this world were the way to reward in the next. The elect were the chosen disciples of God. What better chance of election than success on earth? This was the ethic that provided the foundation for classical economics. In the economist's dusty phrase: each man sought to maximize his own utility.

Charles Darwin wrote his *Origin of the Species* in the 1840s. He argued that all organisms adapted to their environment through a process of natural selection. Only the fittest survived to rear their young, who in turn bore families themselves. Opposition was vocal, but the very people who disagreed with his scientific explanations of animal evolution were the first to apply it to Victorian society. The fittest were those who occupied the leading positions in the community. Life was a struggle, a competitive scramble. And so the social philosophy of the Victorian era was a mixture of the Protestant ethic and the soul of Darwin transmigrated into the body of society.

The first part of the twentieth century has been occupied by a gradual waning of the Victorian ideal of work. America of the 1920s and 1930s, with the huge new flowline factories, was a breeding ground for an entirely new attitude towards man and his new job. The name most widely associated with this change was Frederick Taylor, who has been called the pioneer of scientific management. He has been applauded as the man who made possible the exploitation of the machine so as to maximize its benefit to mankind. Others have reviled him as the man who once said that many jobs in industry could be performed by a trained gorilla. In fact, Frederick Taylor genuinely wanted to help the worker. He felt that the man on the shop floor would be happy with little responsibility and the least complicated task. He felt that man wished to be used efficiently as long as the call upon his intelligence and dexterity was cut to a minimum. But what Taylorism was doing was amputating much of which man is capable. By taking the lowest common denominator he ignored the talents that were ready and waiting to be utilized in industrial processes.

Now in the present age of high mass consumption a new attitude towards earning a living has emerged. The hallmark of this approach is 'to accumulate in order to consume'. I do not think anyone has mapped this out so well as Professor Galbraith* in his own penetrating style. The mental stimulation of work, it is said, has now evaporated. The simple repetitive processes that have to be performed have drained all interest away from everyday work. The pay packet and what it will buy provide the only stimulation to activity.

Today's marketing and advertising techniques — however vital they are in other directions — do tend to reinforce this view. Life does not seem to start until one moves from being a producer to being a consumer. It is good and right that standards of living should rise, that more and more consumer durables should add to the stock of family wealth. But the balance must be tipped back. After all we spend one-third of our life working, one-third in leisure-time activities, and one-third sleeping. We cannot write off one-third of our lives for the sake of another third. This is an unhealthy imbalance.

The philosophy has changed from 'work is good in itself' to work is a necessary means to an end and not something which can provide satisfaction in itself. Now that the Nonconformist ethic has lost its validity we find ourselves in a situation where we no longer have a satisfactory and coherent philosophy about work. But in the present age of vigorous change men and women more than ever need a steady, understandable philosophy to give meaning and purpose to everyday living. Can modern technology provide the setting in which modern man can evolve a modern philosophy of work?

Basically, people work for a wage. Men will work if they are paid; men will work better if the physical conditions are right; they will work better still if their job provides the means of their own mental refinement and growth. Modern technology, unlike the old technologies of the Industrial Revolution, provides an opportunity to create these conditions. We now have the means to contrive and control the working environment so that work can be much more attractive and interesting.

* *The Affluent Society* (Hamish Hamilton, 1958).

The famous Hawthorne Studies between 1927 and 1932 at the Western Electric Company in America showed that giving men and women the minimum to do did not, at the end of the day, show results. They were basically unhappy and as a result they restricted their work. Rather than be a heavily serviced and protected machine, man would on the whole prefer to be treated as a being with the power of thought and decision. This simple fact was discovered when a group of social scientists experimented with the environment in which a group of workers performed their tasks. They found that whatever they did in terms of changing jobs, seating arrangements, lighting, etc., the group of workers under study always improved their performance. And in the end they concluded that they consistently did better because they were being treated as if they were important. This opened up the Promised Land for the academics, and industrial sociology has been Canaan for them ever since.

At this point it is right to look at the constraints of our society and present technology and seek out the difficulties in our system of production which make satisfaction at work, except for the few, a very partial experience. After looking at these physical and external factors, we must then look at the man himself to see if it is possible to provide means for him to develop a fuller experience of life. Is it possible to find ways and means by which every man can achieve self-fulfilment in work?

The size of the productive unit, the speed and rhythm of working with machines, the necessary system of instructions and discipline, the drawbacks of working in what may be unpleasant or even dangerous conditions, and the fear that the skills carefully built up over a lifetime may be made rudely redundant by technological change, are all factors which play upon the human situation in industry.

In the early part of the so-called Industrial Revolution, manufacturing took place in numerous specialist workshops. These workshops could be fairly small in size and in them it was possible for the owner to know personally every one of his workmen and, if he wanted, to exercise a humane influence. Later techniques pulled the work of the workshops into one integrated process under a single roof. Integration was achieved by the slow-moving conveyor belt and automatic, now computerized, controls.

The development of the use of the computer in automatic process control reinforces the economic and other forces which are driving industry into ever larger and more complicated units. The first generation of computers simply provided a data processing service. These expensive machines could sometimes be shared so the smaller company could enjoy the benefits of a data processing service and yet still remain small.

However, the expensive trappings of automated process control cannot be shared. The computer necessarily has to become an integral part of the engineering side of production and only the large company has the throughput to support the extra capital costs and high degree of scientific know-how involved. Modern technology, therefore, impels us towards larger and larger business units, re-fashioning the organizations in which modern man earns his living. The danger is that men may feel they are submerged in vast, mindless corporations. No one works well in the sluggish environment of a sprawling bureaucracy in which the individual loses his sense of identity and purpose and his awareness of the overall pattern of operations.

The development of more precise and sophisticated paperwork, and in particular the use of mathematical techniques in operational research, have meant that the span of managerial control is multiplying fast. The task of controlling a large number of different complicated processes has evolved into a new skill of its own, based upon an entirely new set of rules. Management science is really the science of size. The growth of management as an academic discipline, the establishment of the business schools and the acceleration of interest in management techniques have gone hand-in-hand with the increasing size of the manufacturing unit.

39

The size of the firm and its effect on morale is no new problem: Aristotle suggested that a community would only be stable if it was small enough for everyone to 'know one another's characters'. But the problem is now a growing one. The harsh geometry of the vast organization chart is not enough to explain to ordinary people their place in the procession of production.

No one would suggest that we should become machine breakers and carve up the great corporations. The pay-off in terms of efficiency is too valuable to forego. A demolition job would not help anyone. Indeed the large corporation with all its varied ramifications provides the possibility of research and experiment into the development of personnel and work policies which maximize job satisfaction.

The practice of working with continuously operating machines was an entirely new technology when the factory system was first established. For the first time, man renounced his individual right to set the speed of his own work. This did not necessarily make him a slave. Far from it: often men were released from a heavy burden of physical labour. Even so, working with machines can lead to profound monotony when a relatively small number of simple jobs have to be performed over and over again.

Right at the beginning of the machine age, John Stuart Mill foresaw the dangers of this type of boredom. Writing about the dangers of industrialism, he deplored 'the dull unexciting monotony of their lives ... the absence of any marked individuality ... the narrow mechanized understanding produced by a life spent in executing by fixed rules a fixed task'. This is a description of the dangers rather than the facts as they are today. However, automation and modern technology are quite likely to produce a number of boring jobs that simply have to be performed. So, like the problem of size, the monotony effect of machines on human beings is likely to grow more serious. I believe that the mounting number of industrial disputes in some industries cannot all be laid at the door of discontent with wages. 'Bore-

40

dom money' without exactly being specified joins the long list of discontent payments such as dirt money, danger money, dust money, wet-working money, hot-work money, cold-work money and many others that abound. The inconveniences that all these represent to the worker are not easy to pin down and eradicate, as cash takes the edge off the discomfort.

The command structure of industry, too, provides its own difficulties. Modern technology demands the careful integration of numerous precisely defined and measured operations. Central co-ordination is growing. But where instructions are given there is bound to be friction. Our national philosophy of individualism encourages each man to strive to become master of his own destiny. The discipline of a large and complex organization is therefore bound to appear to the individual as a restraint of the free flight of his own will. Conflict within the firm between managers and men does not arise solely from the bosses' ownership of the factory. The experience of nationalized industry has shown that conflict now arises mainly because some people manage and other people are managed. This is one of the facts of present-day industrial life and it is largely immaterial whether the bosses own the assets or not.

I know there are many who feel that management's principal role is a technical engineering job. But it is the manager's job to create the conditions in which men can develop a satisfactory attitude towards their work. Much can be done by management to reduce the negative effect of the huge organization and the tedious rhythm of working with plodding machines. We can do this through a careful scrutiny of communications and consultation, by designing a safe and acceptable working environment, through measures to make work more interesting, and by a thorough review of the wages system. Above all good communications are a necessary precondition.

There is more than one type of communication. Firstly there are those that concern the organizational efficiency of the enterprise. It is essential to make absolutely sure that policies agreed at the top, through honest discussion, wise counsel and shrewd judgment, are transmitted clearly and effectively to those people who are actually engaged on the job.

The cornerstone of good communications is the knowledge that each man has of the job he is doing and why he is doing it. Communications should be swift enough for decisions to be taken and implemented quickly. They must be accurate and simple enough to survive their passage through the organization, i.e., they must be so designed that they cannot be misused. Instructions can often come in handy as a stick to beat the chap below; alternatively they can be used to put pressure on the level above by working to rule.

The second type of communication is harder. It is difficult to explain clearly the wider context in which the business operates, particularly in an environment in which the techniques of production are changing at a bewildering rate.

The role of the trades unions in the job of communications is a crucial one. It is they who can express the views of the labour force in its most coherent form, and the manager should regard the trades union as an essential point of contact with the men.

When a new production process is developed, no manager can expect to anticipate all the human problems that will be created. More than anything else, in a situation of technological change he must always keep the doors open to the trades unions, because very often they are the bearers of information of which he would otherwise be completely unaware.

Democracy at Westminster has built up a long and distinguished history. Democracy in industry is still in its infancy. As I have stated previously, the essence of democracy is the right of every man's views to be given fair consideration and for no man's opinions to be suppressed. True joint consultation in industry implies the right of every man to express a view and for this to be given honest and unbiased consideration. The best way of finding out what a man wants is to ask him, and joint consultation recognizes this simple fact.

Consultative meetings should never be allowed to become a drab routine where the main item on the agenda is the Minutes of the last meeting. Unless consultation is a living element within an organization, feelings may be bottled up and an explosion might easily take place in the form of industrial action. In the technological restlessness of our time, consultation must take on a dynamic role: innovation is built into our community and individuals must be reassured and enabled to understand the meaning of technological change for them.

On top of this is the fear that the industrial system may finally reject a man's skills. As the speed of change quickens so skills grow obsolete more rapidly. Technical change will demand a radical re-grouping of the range of skills required. More and more it has become plainly evident that to compete successfully internationally an increasing number of mergers of companies will take place and substantial rationalization must result. This will add further impetus to the speed of change. Mergers will, in the short term, make fewer jobs, but will make possible the investment of substantial capital investment in the new techniques which are available now, waiting to be exploited.

At this moment of time the turn-over of skills has still a long way to go. At the moment three-quarters of the labour force have changed the nature of their jobs only once, or not at all, during the last ten years. But, clearly, as the technological dynamism of our time gathers momentum this situation will change. It will have to be accepted that some people may be called upon to change skills several times in their lifetime.

Perhaps the leading cause of industrial mistrust lies in the wages system. Yet the amount of friction and heat generated by wage negotiations can be reduced if management and men accept a number of simple propositions. The first thing that is needed is frankness on all sides. Wage negotiations today are often little more than a ritual clog dance. Managers should be prepared to open their books to the unions. Then negotiations can take place in the clear light of accepted facts.

Much is said about the need for incentives for industrial workers in the form of piecework. In a modern age I cannot agree. Piecework is the wages system of the pick and shovel, the hand-loom, the hammer and anvil. Men now work to the speed of continuously operating machines. Piecework is a mischief-maker in a modern situation like this, and can quickly become the playground for all sorts of intrigues. Piecework can never become the alternative to good management, and so long as piecework persists it will certainly be a brake on managerial innovation and a constant source of inflationary wages creep and industrial discontent.

A minority of employers have the habit of using wage increases to buy off trouble. Instead of trying to understand the complexities of human relations in a situation of technical change, they are content to concede an increase in wages rates whenever trouble occurs. The net result is the buying and selling of restrictive practices and a sad distortion of the national wages system. The aim should surely be to create a structure providing acceptable scales of rewards in which groups of men are related to each other according to their responsibilities and specialized requirements. Piecework is the negation of this kind of logical basis and produces a wage structure which in most cases has little reference to equity or fairness.

There is a strong case for more research into the effects of different working environments and the consequences of working with various materials and machines. Modern technology is revolutionizing the working environment and work processes and it is now much easier to make these acceptable from the human point of view, by making use of the collective wisdom of the work-study expert, the design engineer and the ergonomist.

As the type of industrial work changes, we in industry shall have to learn much more of the capabilities of the human mind and body. As the number of people employed to monitor machines begins to expand, we need to know more about man's power of concentration. We need, for example, to know the best type of indication equipment so that human responses can be quick and effective. We have to watch carefully that human beings are fitted and trained for the jobs they do if angry frustration is to be avoided. Where boring jobs have to be done we must try to implant variety through job rotation schemes and measures to secure job enlargement.

The techniques of scientific management must be exploited to ensure that the meaningless snippets of work into which most industrial processes are divided add up to a meaningful whole. By this means management can inject life and interest into a dead working environment. Together with good communications, a just and understandable wages system, a healthy work environment and research into the physical and mental capabilities of men, such measures can create a satisfying working environment. What is needed is nothing less than a revolution: in themselves more welfare benefits, bigger bonuses, safer and more hygienic working conditions will not provide happiness or fulfilment in industrial society.

If we are to foster a new attitude towards work, and find something to replace present widespread notions that men work only in order to consume the products of modern technology, it is essential to create the conditions in which a producer's philosophy, not a consumer's philosophy, of work can grow. This is not a case of retreating into a study, reading ancient volumes and penning a philosophical treatise. I mean the sort of philosophy which is acceptable to the majority of work-people: a philosophy in which work provides interest and fulfilment. We cannot return to the ideal of the medieval craftsman, but we can surely do much to give work a new meaning.

While this is a difficult and delicate task I believe it can be done. I have suggested that one way is through good communications, which keep men and women in touch with the

45

wider situation. Others are through a radical review of the wages structure, the use of re-training facilities and the use of schemes for job rotation and job enlargement.

Finally, I am quite clear in my own mind that all this is management's responsibility. This, of course, is not all and certainly not the hardest part of their task. The most difficult job of all is to provide self-fulfilment at work so that the total man can be devoted to his job. We have only just lifted the corner of this veil. We must look at each job and ask ourselves whether a man's career allows him to maintain his individuality, to create new ideas, to grow in knowledge and to solve the maze of problems with which he is presented. Clearly the opportunities of doing this amongst higher management are much more apparent than for the worker at his bench. There is no easy formula. But one can break into the circle by the careful training of all who supervise others at whatever level. They need to understand the man as well as the job. The human being can be 'engineered' towards this self-fulfilment.

Men who can fire others with enthusiasm and imagination are unfortunately sadly few and far between, and while there is still far to go in providing the right environment, the job of treating people in industry as human beings has hardly been begun. Again this is a job for management. Human engineering in the broadest sense is the job of the bosses and always has been. It is their responsibility to ensure that proper expert advice is sought. Industry would do well to accept more fully the talent that lies within the professions that hitherto have remained outside the mainstream of industrial life. By becoming more closely involved these professions could well help to solve a much wider range of human problems.

I would instance, as an extreme case, a profession not normally regarded as having much to do with business management: the medical profession. Doctors have the skill and the concern that could make them a powerful force for good if opportunities were opened up for them. Industrial medical care has already produced splendid results. But by being brought closer to the backbone of industrial management, doctors could add to their range of professional skill and knowledge and so enrich their own work. Industry has been quite prepared to accept the doctor's work in treating the consequences of industrial accidents. But it might be more rewarding if the medical profession could be brought in with the ergonomist at a much earlier stage, when machines are being designed and men are being fitted into a mechanical situation. More often than not it is the work-study expert, or the design engineer—an electrical or mechanical engineer—who designs machines for men to work with.

As the type of industrial work begins to change we shall have to learn much more of the capabilities of the human mind and the human body. A combination of ergonomics and medical skill could be dynamic. Here the medical profession could make a profound contribution. For the medical officer concerned it would mean an emphasis on the preventative medicine and ergonomics fields and a movement away from the traditional clinical approach. But this could be a very rewarding shift of interest for medical officers and industry alike.

Doctors are already doing fine work in the choice of work for disabled men undergoing re-training, examining new entrants and recommending the type of work for which they are suited, and providing an everyday treatment service. Industry now needs to accept that medical officers can also help in designing the optimal working environment. In all this, I am convinced it is not the medical profession which is holding back: there is a reluctance on the part of industry generally to recognize that the doctor's skills can be extended and used in new ways.

This is only one example of a profession which could contribute much to industry. Something similar could be said of other professions: architects, lawyers, etc., all have something to contribute, beyond the role they presently play, to fashion a humane and efficient working environment.

47

It is only in an industrial framework with men working harmoniously together that a new work philosophy can begin to emerge. It is also absolutely fair to say that unless the economic climate is a buoyant and confident one, there is no hope of any worthwhile philosophy emerging. Economic stagnation is barren ground for any philosophy which contains an element of hope, and it has already been demonstrated how easy it is to talk ourselves into that particular barren ground.

I think we must sensibly conclude that work can neither bring man nearer God, nor should it serve as a punishment meted out by an angry Creator. What it can do is to provide a means whereby the individual finds a place in society and a method by which he can stimulate his mind and look after his physical requirements. These are broadly the three principles with which this chapter opened: the idea that most moral codes can be distilled into providing for the physical needs of man—food, shelter, warmth; the social needs, of family and good fellowship; and the mental needs of self-fulfilment.

The idea of work as the provider of social solidarity (and indeed conflict) in society is most closely associated with Marxist thinking. Here at least Marx was right; the job a man does, how it relates to the activities of others, goes a long way towards giving him an appreciation of the part he plays in society. When each man did everything for himself in the old peasant societies, he could see quite clearly why he must labour. It was he who directly produced the food, found the clothing and built the house for his family. But in the sophisticated division of labour that exists today no man produces the whole of the goods and services he and his family need. Very often he may be producing something which neither he nor his family would wish to use. He may be producing a tiny portion of a large item: a portion that may seem quite insignificant when he considers the whole. Work and the needs of daily living have therefore diverged quite markedly, and the direct production

48

of goods and services can no longer be the raison d'être of work for the man and his family.

Today, in answer to the question 'Who are you?', most people would, after their name, give their occupation. This is the description that fits a man into his social context, that pins him into his place in the community. The first element in any philosophy of work must be that the job a man does names him as a member of the team.

What of those whose occupations grant them a pretty low status in the eyes of their fellow men? These tasks, although they are unpleasant (such as refuse disposal) or even just unpopular (such as income tax inspection), are all just as vital to the smooth running of society. I do not deplore or sneer at people in occupations who choose to change their names in the 'rat-catcher to rodent official' category. This is all to the good if it makes the job more acceptable. But in the long run the problem will have to be solved by nothing short of a revolution in social attitudes. If a new and satisfactory work philosophy is to be established, then each man must see that the part his job plays in the whole and the job done by every other individual is both honourable and socially useful. This requires a more democratic, less snobbish society based upon a frank acceptance of the place that every man has. In education it may mean that we should pursue a policy of non-segregation. But whatever social changes we need to make, the warning is clear that if a work philosophy is to be based upon the status and identity a job gives to a man in the community, then we shall have to ensure that every useful role is an honourable one too.

Turning from the role of work in society and social solidarity, another element is the part that work plays in physical and mental well-being. The connection with physical well-being is fairly plain to see. Wages produce most of the things the individual and his family need. This is done either through direct purchase or through the collective provision of certain services in the fields of welfare, education, defence and transport, which are covered by taxation. The role of work in the mental well-being of the individual is much less straightforward. The mental well-being of the man in industry has been the goal of most of the discussion that has taken place. If one principle of a new work philosophy is to be the mental stimulation it provides, then radical changes will have to take place in the way in which we arrange work and the working environment. A man must be adequately trained in his duties so that his mind can be applied to the way in which he carries out his task. Communications must be good enough to spark off his imagination and interest. Job enlargement can infuse permanent interest into an otherwise narrow, crabbed and unrewarding duty. If we treat men like machines, then we quite naturally slip into the trap of deciding that the narrower the range of duties then the more likely an individual is to be an expert and carry out his duties efficiently. This is a misconception.

A new work philosophy, based on the notion that work places man in society and provides for mental and physical well-being, requires a society which is willing to change itself in order to do better. This is why a new philosophy of work and human engineering are fastened closely together. Human engineering creates the conditions in which a new work philosophy can be followed. It is a philosophy such as this that releases the full potential of human beings.

By placing this new philosophy in the centre of the discussion on human engineering, the human element in Britain is placed in the centre of the discussion of this country's long-term future.

Britain, concentrating its attention once again on the element that really matters, the human element, armed with a new philosophy of work, could become once again a front runner in the nations of the world: the qualities of the people of Britain first set the world on fire and though in recent years the spark has dimmed, the opportunity now arises for it to burst into life again.

The people of Britain will respond readily, if the fine skill, effort and concentration which is put into the engineering of a computer or a satellite is put into human engineering. It will not come by rules, regulations, controls and statutes and certainly not from pontifical speeches by politicians in Parliament and elsewhere or from the quiet decisions of the nameless and faceless ones in Whitehall.

3 The Personnel Manager

It is strange but I believe generally true that the most neglected aspect of industrial activity throughout the years has been the human and personal problems of people at their place of employment. The reason for this is not far to seek. Work-people in the nineteenth century and well into the twentieth were traditionally hired and fired as the exigencies of the business demanded, and while there was a pool of unemployment, men from whom to choose, the utter waste and the human tragedies that ensued were of little consequence to the employers.

Nor did the early capitalists feel that the office staff required humane treatment. The personnel policies for the Victorian counting-house were almost as harsh as for the factory floor. A document entitled 'Office Staff Practice' was issued to a group of office workers at Lichfield in 1852 and is worth quoting in full:

1. Godliness, cleanliness and punctuality are the necessities of a good business.
2. This firm has reduced the hours of work and the clerical staff will now only have to be present between the hours of 7 a.m. and 6 p.m. on weekdays.
3. Daily prayers will be held each morning in the main office. The clerical staff will be present.
4. Clothing must be of a sober nature. The clerical staff will not disport themselves in raiment of bright colours, nor will they wear hose, unless in good repair.

5. Overshoes and top-coats may not be worn in the office, but neck scarves and headwear may be worn in inclement weather.

6. A stove is provided for the benefit of the clerical staff; coal and wood must be kept in the locker. It is recommended that each member of the clerical staff bring four pounds of coal, each day, during cold weather.

7. No member of the clerical staff may leave the room without permission from Mr Rogers. The calls of nature are permitted, and clerical staff may use the garden below the second gate. This area must be kept in good order.

8. No talking is allowed during business hours.

9. The craving of tobacco, wines or spirits is a human weakness, and, as such, is forbidden to all members of the clerical staff.

10. Now that the hours of business have been drastically reduced the partaking of food is allowed between 11.30 a.m. and noon, but work will not, on any account, cease.

11. Members of the clerical staff will provide their own pens. A new sharpener is available, on application to Mr Rogers.

12. Mr Rogers will nominate a senior clerk to be responsible for the cleanliness of the main office and the private office, and all boys and juniors will report to him 40 minutes before prayers, and will remain after closing hours for similar work. Brushes, brooms, scrubbers and soap are provided by the owners.

13. The new increased weekly wages are as detailed hereunder —

Junior boys
(to 11 years)   —1/4d Boys (to 14 years)— 2/1d
Juniors   —4/8d Junior Clerks   — 8/7d

Clerks		—10/9d Senior Clerks
		(after 15 years
		with the owners) —21/-d

> The owners recognize the generosity of the new Labour
> Laws, but will expect a great rise in output of work
> to compensate for these near-Utopian conditions.

Poor Mr Rogers: what it must have been to be chief of
personnel in those days.

Not until the Second World War was it thoroughly understood that the misuse of the nation's most precious asset could
not be permitted to go on in this way. There was an awareness
too that the aftermath of the First World War could not and
would not be tolerated. No one saw this more clearly than
Ernest Bevin who, when he became Minister of Labour in
1940, not only set about the task of mobilizing labour in the
all-out war effort but, with an eye to post-war requirements,
organized it in such a way that there could be no return to
pre-war neglect of the conditions of people at their place of
employment. A large number of joint councils of one kind and
another grew under his persuasion, and in many cases representatives of work-people and employers met for the first time
to discuss mutual problems. The lead that Bevin gave was
eagerly seized upon by both employers and trade union leaders,
and he had the immense satisfaction of seeing his ideas, based
upon his massive experience as a trade union leader, come
nearer to fruition.

Despite the fact that industrial disputes, largely of an unofficial character, dominate the headlines of industrial life, it
would be a pity if one did not note the tremendous improvement in industrial relations in these post-war years. The sensa-
tional publicity given to some disputes should not be allowed
to disguise the real progress which has been made in this field.

In the twenty years between the wars the number of days
lost in disputes was 400,000,000. In the twenty post-war years

it was 60,000,000. A notable advance; but bearing in mind that the pre-war figures were mainly strikes of an official nature, including the 1926 General Strike, the real change has been that the majority of days lost post-war were of an unofficial nature and, with some notable exceptions, in strikes of short duration. They arose, therefore, not because of differences between trade unions and employers or employers' associations, but because of local disagreements, usually involving groups of people at their place of employment.

The scene has changed. No longer powerful antagonists at battle stations over a wide area, but group disturbance in factory and workshop which the employer and the trade union did not want but could not contain. This more than anything else has emphasized the importance of ensuring that the bush fires are prevented, and if they do occur that they are put out promptly without causing damage.

Today it is insufficient attention to the field of personnel problems and the failure to apply known techniques of personnel management which so often provide the harvest of industrial strife. There are many progressive employers who can testify to the benefits that have flowed as a result of special attention to personnel problems. Perhaps the mining industry is the most striking example. We need not go back to the inter-war years, although the student looking at those figures would wonder what hope there was in those days of ever seeing industrial peace in mining. It is only necessary to look at the years since the war.

The table on page 56 shows the total number of stoppages in the mining industry, compared with the rest of the economy.

This table shows the startling change in the number of disputes in what has always been regarded as an exceptionally strike-prone industry. In coal-mining the number of stoppages has decreased rapidly, and with it the amount of coal lost: in 1968 the days lost were less than a quarter of those lost ten years earlier and arising from the disputes the amount of coal lost was less than 300,000 tons. The main reason why the number of disputes has fallen is that since nationalization it has been possible to bring a much closer association between management and worker to bear upon industrial relations at the actual place of work. More recently, the introduction of a day-wage structure in place of piecework for faceworkers has supplemented this factor.

United Kingdom—Number of Stoppages due to Industrial Disputes,
1946–67

	Number of Stoppages			
Year	*Coal Mining*	*Tons Lost*	*In the rest of the economy*	*Altogether*
1946	1,339	769,800	866	2,205
1947	1,066	1,643,500	655	1,721
1948	1,125	955,800	634	1,759
1949	879	1,409,200	547	1,426
1950	861	967,200	478	1,339
1951	1,067	1,013,300	652	1,719
1952	1,226	1,716,700	488	1,714
1953	1,313	1,148,400	433	1,746
1954	1,466	1,506,800	523	1,989
1955	1,784	3,180,700	635	2,419
1956	2,078	2,146,500	570	2,648
1957	2,226	1,826,700	633	2,859
1958	1,964	1,450,800	665	2,629
1959	1,311	972,900	1,592	2,903
1960	1,669	1,558,600	1,163	2,832
1961	1,466	2,064,000	1,220	2,686
1962	1,207	1,123,400	1,242	2,449
1963	993	1,319,100	1,075	2,068
1964	1,063	1,330,400	1,461	2,524
1965	743	1,276,900	1,611	2,354
1966	556	1,821,600	1,381	1,937
1967	394	496,600*	1,722	2,116
1968	219	287,400	2,131	2,350

Sources: Department of Employment and Productivity (Number of stoppages — D.E.P. basis of inclusion)
National Coal Board (tons lost — all disputes)
* Piecework replaced by day wage for coal face workers from 1966.

It is also clear from the table, however, that while the number of industrial disputes taking place in the mining industry has been substantially reduced, disputes in other parts of the economy have risen so that overall the total number remains roughly the same. Although, as I have said, some progress has been made, a great deal remains to be done in some industries.

The measurement of days lost in disputes is of course only the tip of the iceberg in relation to the damage done to the national economy. The bad feeling that results at every level between management and men lives on and shows itself in failure to co-operate, and a readiness to flare up on the least provocation, all to the detriment of the company or industry concerned. The real price that is paid for failures in the effective use of personnel management techniques in industry is difficult to quantify. Undoubtedly the slow growth in the economy is one of the disastrous results.

How many potential gains are being lost by the failure to take full advantage of the rapid technical advances which are now possible? Is the failure to obtain the maximum machine use from high capital cost equipment not one of the problems in our failure to lower costs? The 'go-slow' is often worse than a strike, and over-manning is an economic crime. More production is, I am sure, lost by the inefficient use of labour than by direct industrial strife. There are no figures to prove this, but one has only to talk to trade union leaders and leaders of industry to appreciate that this is so.

The time is rapidly approaching when the investment cost of new machinery will not be justified except by a twenty-one-shift week, round-the-clock working all day and every day. In oil refineries, power stations, gas, steel, the public services and all utilities this is commonplace enough. Shift work and week-end work are operated in these industries because they are a must. Life could not go on unless electricity, gas, transport, entertainment and food services were available in what is generally regarded as out-of-work hours. There would be no milk on Monday mornings if the farming community worked a five-day week. However, economic pressures are now increasingly extending shift working beyond the provision of public services because of the need to operate expensive machinery round the clock, thus bringing an increasing number of people into the cycle of continuous working. This will inevitably extend still further in the course of time, but, to succeed, one should always be well in front of the inevitable. Letting events shape our ends will only provide a living; anticipating the inevitable, setting the lead, as we did in the Industrial Revolution, will give us pride of place, high standards of living and the wherewithal to help the newly emerging nations of the world.

Good industrial relations are not just a question of preventing industrial strife and the downing of tools, but a necessary requirement to maximize the use of working time. To neglect this aspect of management, or to do it imperfectly, is to neglect the most potent force we possess. And this is a field that has not yet been exploited to the full. Vast expenditure and close managerial oversight is given to research and development for technical advancement. The same high degree of managerial oversight is essential in dealing with people in industry, and in this field special skills and training are just as important as in the more technical fields. Highly qualified and skilled personnel managers are urgently required in industry to provide line management with the very best advice and assistance in dealing with this most complex and emotive field in managerial decision-making.

The need has been evident for years, but the establishment of personnel managers has been a long time coming to industry. Even today, although there are 40,000 plants in Britain with over twenty-five employees, probably not more than a half have adequately trained personnel managers. In many firms someone is just deputed to look after personnel matters as part of another job; in others someone is appointed without first being trained.

Sometimes a trade union official is persuaded to come on to the management side of industry as a personnel manager or labour relations manager. While the trade union official is first-class material for the making of a good personnel officer, it is a mistake to assume that without further training his experience in his former role is sufficient to enable him to carry out successfully all the functions of really competent personnel work. Indeed, the present escalation of many personnel problems in industry, leading to disputes which need never have happened, is often caused by the folly of appointing a man or a woman because they 'get on well with the workers', or have been particularly active in the trade union, or the social side of the factory or plant life. Background experience of this kind is undoubtedly valuable, but is only the raw material from which a really well-qualified personnel manager can be fashioned.

The reason for this kind of appointment, followed by training on the job, is not far to seek. It is a natural corollary of the way personnel management found its way into industry. It began in the years before the First World War in the field of welfare. Since the days of Robert Owen in the first half of the nineteenth century, if not before, there have always been progressive and liberal-minded employers who were genuinely interested in the welfare of their employees. This was not simply self-interest, although it was always appreciated by a few that a happy and contented staff did much to improve the atmosphere and efficiency of a factory or workshop. In Owen's case, at least, it derived from a genuine and deep human interest in people and from a strongly held belief that an employer must bear some responsibility for the people he employed, quite apart from the payment of wages for work done. Nevertheless, this was quite a departure from the normal practice, particularly in the days when a measure of unemployment and the immobility of labour created no incentive to depart from the then almost universal hire and fire principles.

59

First efforts in this field were directed mainly towards women and young persons' welfare, and in the main women were appointed as welfare officers. The forerunner of the present Institute of Personnel Management was set up in 1913 as the Association of Industrial Welfare Officers.

Then came the war of 1914–18 and as men went to the trenches their places in the factories, and particularly the munition factories, were taken by a growing army of women. In 1916 the Ministry of Munitions established the Industrial Welfare Department, which in turn led to the foundation of the Industrial Welfare Society in 1918 and the National Institute of Industrial Psychology in 1921.

The whole emphasis of these activities lay in the direction of welfare in the traditional sense, but they also clearly indicated the need to seek out and take care of the needs of individuals at their place of work. Welfare, labour relations and wage negotiations began to be seen as a whole, and there was a recognition that pure welfare could not be divorced from the whole. It was thus not a far cry from university studies in social science, and the appointment of personnel managers in industry.

However, it was the Second World War, which brought with it the Essential Works Order, which finally pointed unmistakably to the importance and, indeed, the absolute requirement for someone to specialize in and take care of labour problems.

Today the scope for the adequately trained personnel manager has widened. While it is true that different firms allocate different fields of operation, and different levels in management, to the personnel manager, and there is not yet universal agreement on the precise role he has to play, there is a growing realization that people in industry need to have special, detailed and day-to-day consideration if this essential asset is to be utilized to the best advantage of the individual and the company as a whole.

There can by now surely be no doubts about the importance of recognizing the human and social implications of the whole range of managerial decisions and policies. A decision in the boardroom, for example, to deal with redundancy, short-term working or mobility of labour on strictly commercial grounds would be unthinkable, without careful analysis and detailed thought in relation to its impact on the individuals affected and the group of workers as a whole. A very careful plan of action needs to be prepared, which takes personal consequences into consideration in the most minute detail, before any such policy decisions can be successfully applied. Even then, such is the variety of domestic circumstance in human beings, there will be unforeseen problems, and however few there may be, failure to have the machinery to deal with them promptly and effectively could lead, if not to total failure, certainly to partial failure which could seriously affect the whole operation.

The personnel manager must therefore, in my view, rank high in the managerial hierarchy. This is acknowledged in many large firms where the position warrants membership of the board of directors. But whether a member of the board or not, it is essential for the personnel manager to be present when policy decisions are being conceived. The role of the personnel manager is one of peculiar difficulty because the administration of personnel policies, which he has recommended, is necessarily a line management responsibility. Down the line, management can quite easily look down their noses at the advice tendered, perhaps even think in derisory terms of 'mollycoddling' or 'I'm the boss, work-people should do as they're told.' But if it is recognized that the personnel manager has access to the very highest level, and that top-line management at that level has discussed and included in its plans and policies the advice of the personnel manager, then the possibility of line management at lower levels thinking that such advice is an intrusion recedes and the advice becomes more acceptable, if not sought after.

Modern management can no longer be regarded as a purely technical operation. The operations with which management must be concerned are legion, but none of them can be

61

conducted without people. The acme of good management is to succeed in bringing people of all kinds and dispositions to work happily together with the maximum of efficiency and co-operation and the minimum of discomfort. To succeed in this calls for high qualities of leadership, bearing in mind that the make-up of the factory floor is in teams and groups. It must be appreciated that few people work for the company name. They work for their immediate managerial superior and with their immediate colleagues. People work for people and not an institution. No company is likely to be completely successful unless the influence of the specialist in human relations, the personnel manager or his equivalent, is felt in a personal way by the individual worker both direct and through general management right down the line to the foreman or supervisor and through them to the worker.

Considerably more money, effort and time is put into machine development than into understanding and developing people. This is not to say that effort can be measured by time and money, but management which stints the effort to understand and develop its work-force is neglecting its most valuable asset. The success of personnel administration can be measured by the degree of ready co-operation that is induced between management and those who are managed. Such co-operation will not come by the carrot and stick act, with the carrot a bonus for extra effort, or the stick of unemployment for failure to co-operate. It can only come if there is a clear appreciation that a special relationship must exist between management and worker and that if the relationship is right and production and administration go smoothly then the financial results ensuing represent an ever-increasing improvement in rewards.

The personnel manager must in addition to his own skills be familiar with the technical problems of line management. Planning is the order of the day in any successful enterprise. Planning by business objectives lends a new meaning to production planning, capital investment planning, machine design, product development and marketing. These are all facets of the business which the personnel manager must understand, if he is to give worthwhile and acceptable advice to the technical manager.

In treating the work-force as individuals and as groups, the personnel manager must make a very careful study of every dispute. Too often after a dispute, large or small, the file is closed with a sigh of relief and the way cleared for the next battle. But the file may have been closed before conclusions have been drawn which should be applied to similar situations elsewhere or which might prevent the same dispute from breaking out again. The necessity for analysing all the causes of disputation and the day-by-day turn of events cannot be over-stated.

It is a mistake to think that men like to strike; it is an even bigger mistake to think that communist agitators can create strikes for political reasons. It is true that for political reasons the agitator will try to engender a strike in all countries except those governed by communists; there is little doubt too that the agitator will keep the pot boiling when a strike is on. But the genesis of every strike is a grievance and very often a genuine one. In many cases the grievance that sparks off the strike is not the more serious underlying cause but 'the last straw that breaks the camel's back'. The detailed analysis of every dispute, therefore, whether it leads to strike action or not, must be studied with great care. Deep-seated grievances which may well be minor in character can be, and indeed very often are, the seeds from which the harvest of bad industrial relations is reaped.

Once men know that management is ready and anxious to deal effectively and promptly with problems and take such administrative action as may be necessary to prevent the same or similar problems arising, they will be more forthcoming in the earlier stages of a grievance and thus provide an opportunity to nip trouble in the bud. As in all other walks of life, the trade union contains within it men who are dissidents, natural trouble-makers, and constantly anti-management, but they are a tiny minority. The heart of the trade union movement is sound and its purpose and policy transparently clear.

It is regarded as natural, in fact essential, for management to use all their resources of intelligence and administrative ability to make a profit. Why should it be regarded as questionable for the trade union similarly to use every fair device and tactic to achieve its legitimate end: to secure the best wages and conditions it can possibly get for its members? The objective should be for management to make it abundantly clear to the trade union, and the rank and file members on the shop floor in particular, that their best personal interests are served by helping to increase profits by co-operative effort. It is only out of increased profitability brought about by increased productivity and the elimination of waste that a steady improvement in wages and conditions can be obtained without raising prices, thus keeping the market for the product and ensuring continuity of employment.

The personnel manager must make it apparent at all costs that he is not an anti-union tool of management. In the United States particularly, and in some countries on the Continent, this has been the trade union criticism of personnel management. Indeed, one of the main tasks of personnel management is to ensure that far from being anti-union, line management is properly advised as to the assistance which could and should be given to the shop steward and the unions to do their jobs effectively at plant level. Adequate facilities for union representatives to do their jobs with thoroughness are essential if co-operation with management is to be smooth.

A well-run trade union organization at plant level, operating openly without 'hole in the corner' conspiracy, is mutually advantageous to both worker and management. Every decision of management has an impact upon the employee, and the choice is not whether the effect upon the worker should be studied or ignored, but whether the consequence of the impact should be considered carefully by the specialist in personnel management or be taken up by line management as part of their already multitudinous and onerous tasks.

A factory must be adequately manned, and the manpower adequately trained. This might properly be regarded as the primary responsibility of personnel management. Manpower budgeting is essential to adequate and economical staffing, and will indicate the correct recruitment policy. Careful selection is a vital factor in the building up of a balanced labour force, and with this goes the proper introduction to the company to ensure that the new employee is made aware of its aims and organization. The provision of adequate welfare facilities, social activities and retirement schemes today are all commonplace in modern management, but they need to be carefully considered and thought out, I suggest by a properly trained professional personnel manager.

Promotion prospects loom very large in the minds of progressive young people coming into industry; management should always know the composition of their second and third teams, and have the means of smoothly filling vacancies in the top echelons from people adequately trained and eager to accept increased responsibilities. This necessitates the maintenance of detailed personnel records and careful long-term career planning. The filling of a top vacancy cannot be left to someone's view that 'X is a good man', based very often on limited experience. The personnel manager's records should indicate those who are qualified by reference to their progress and training throughout their working life, thus providing a sound, well-defined basis on which the personal judgment of the higher executive can be exercised.

The development of wage and salary structures appropriate to each industry is today becoming a much more exacting exercise. In large companies, the repercussions of movements in one field have to be carefully considered. This most sensitive sector of company operations is a subject for continual careful oversight and advice so that no wrong decisions are made, even with the best of intentions.

It is vitally important that correct relations are maintained with trade unions at plant, area and national level. There is a great deal of unwritten but nevertheless important protocol in this of the 'Unto Caesar the things that are Caesar's' type. Feelings and emotions are easily aroused, and to ignore this is fatal.

At plant, area and national levels spheres of authority are reasonably clear, but will not be the same in all unions, some of which tend to centralize power and authority, while others provide within their rules for considerable power and decision-making at the extremities. It is important for the maintenance of good relations that these areas of influence and authority should be clearly understood by the personnel manager and line management alike. Lack of knowledge of these matters which inadvertently leads to communication with the wrong level within the trade union can be disastrous. The shop steward whose managerial superior has by-passed him with a problem and gone directly to a higher level in the union hierarchy can carry a resentment about what he considers as 'going over my head' which can poison relations over a long period. Equally, to try to settle a problem at a lower level than the protocol justifies might give a quick result in the short-term, but the quiet remark of the senior union official 'Why didn't you see me about it?' contains its own warning. This all boils down to knowing with whom to negotiate on the particular matter in hand, and at the same time whom to advise that the negotiation is taking place.

The list of the personnel manager's functions set out above is by no means complete. The establishment of adequate consultative machinery is a must which I need not dwell upon here as a later chapter is specially devoted to its consideration.

Similarly I shall deal later with the need for channels of communication to be created which are clear and precise. Indeed, the whole field of human engineering which is covered by this book is properly the concern of every personnel manager.

The problems arising from the introduction of new technology or administrative techniques are of especial concern to the personnel manager. Changes are constantly being made in working methods because of changes in technology: these in turn will inevitably lead to changes in the administrative organization which have to be handled with infinite care if they are to operate successfully. Clerical and administrative staff now also need to be covered on the same lines that have been established for dealing with the unionized manual and craft worker. This is becoming much more marked as the historic difference between white collar and manual worker is now becoming blurred. The introduction of new techniques of production, the new developments in automation and the use of the computer on a much bigger scale is changing very substantially the ratio between manual and clerical workers. It has been pointed out that the proportion of people engaged in administrative, technical and clerical employment in manufacturing industries in 1935 was 13 per cent; by 1960 it was over 21 per cent; and by 1967, the latest year for which figures are available, the proportion had risen to over 25 per cent. This rise is bound to continue as the techniques now available are exploited and are followed by the even more revolutionary techniques coming off the drawing board. Technical innovation and expansion seems likely to lead eventually in many industries to a virtual abolition of the distinction between the manual and the white-collar worker.

This rise of non-manual workers has already shown itself in the increasing membership of the unions organizing the white-collar workers, affiliated to the T.U.C. and the fall in the numbers in unions in the heavy industries like mining. This of itself is producing a new social shift in industry. The tradition

67

that the manual worker is organized and the administrative worker barely so is fast disappearing and the supervisors, the scientists and the back-room boys generally are now active in trade union organization.

This is a field that will place further burdens and responsibilities upon the personnel manager. The problems that these changes are bound to create must be anticipated and studied, as they add a new dimension to the problem of wages, salaries and conditions. How long can it be, for example, that the farce can go on being played of dividing work-people arbitrarily into workers and staff?

So often one sees the craftsman's daughter straight from school working in the office in the firm where her father works on the factory floor, with far superior conditions of work attached to her job than her father has after many years of service. That these differences will disappear there is no doubt. But how? By long and protracted industrial warfare or by an intelligent recognition of change and with it a planned appreciation as to the way the change can come, with goodwill and the improved productivity to pay for it? Will piece rates and bonusing last for ever? I doubt it.

What kind of change is needed and how can it be programmed? Is the worker going to be brought more into management? If so will it be on the German pattern, where the workers are elected to the supervisory boards?

I wonder whether the fashionable cry for participation will lead to any fundamental change in the relations between workers and management and whether a formula can be found which will really identify the worker with management to any appreciable extent. Perhaps industry would be better off by not pretending that it is humanly possible to bring the worker directly into management decisions and instead providing far superior consultative machinery that would ensure workers' views were fully taken into account before decisions were made. Perhaps it would be better to recognize the basic differences of approach between management and workers and their representatives and try to secure closer co-operation by attention to the real points of mutual interest.

I could go on indicating the changes that are inevitable over the years ahead: some much nearer than many people imagine. Over all lies the task of speedy identification of the vast number of problems that must inevitably arise in a modern industrial society, and their solutions.

In many of these problems, the company will be identified with other companies engaged in similar manufacture or trade, and there specialized representation on employers' associations is called for. Again, there is an important role here for the professional personnel manager.

This account does not by any means cover the full scope of matters involving employees which require detailed expert attention, but at least it indicates the need for specialist-trained people in personnel management. Line management, except in the smallest of firms, cannot hope to handle adequately all these problems while at the same time carrying out its own managerial functions.

The need for the appointment of a personnel manager in all but the smallest of companies therefore is in my view of paramount importance. The scope of the duties covered must necessarily be conditioned by the particular circumstances: because of the variety of activities in production, manufacture, commerce and services, and the varying size of companies in all these fields, it is not possible to lay down a common pattern of organization to handle industrial relations. Each programme must be adapted to the particular needs of the plant. But in my view no progressive management can be without the help, guidance and advice of an expert in these fields. Even the smallest of firms require someone whose primary function it is to handle human relations, even if it is part of the functions of a line manager.

The personnel manager cannot be relegated to a minor role.

He must loom as large in the organization of the company as all other managerial posts of comparable size and importance. He has a difficult part to play and there certainly will be occasions when there is a substantial difference of opinion between him and line management. In the end, it must be recognized that the personnel manager is there to advise, and decisions have to be taken, and differences resolved, by senior management. No one should worry about differences of view on a matter of industrial relations; in fact it is a healthy sign if from time to time a difference of view is expressed for senior management to settle. In industrial relations there is plenty of scope for judgment and timing, and no one can be certain in advance that either one solution or another is absolutely right. A third opinion, and at that level a decisive one, should not be regarded as 'infra dig.', but as quite a normal working out of solutions to human problems.

The personnel manager must take seriously his responsibilities to represent to management the problems of the worker; but he must also make it abundantly clear that he understands the day-to-day problems with which line management is faced. He must recognize that line management is there to make a profit, whether in a privately-owned or state-owned organization. Management must be cost conscious, and while some policies advocated by the personnel manager may well be difficult to quantify, the test of such schemes must be the sound gauge of benefits to the industry.

During this century we have seen a move away from the old idea that managers are 'born', to the concept that they can be 'made' by training and development. This, in the context of the revolution in personnel management techniques, has meant a growing need for professional advice and standards in this field. No management can abdicate its industrial relations functions; nor can it fulfil them effectively without the necessary training.

This need called into being organizations such as the Institute of Personnel Management, which provide a nationwide professional standard of expertise and training. Their publications, courses and membership are now well-established features of the industrial scene, which indicates the real progress made since the days when management and unions alike regarded them with indifference or suspicion. But while the professional personnel manager is accepted, his role in the increasingly important field of human engineering will continue to grow and require the development of further techniques and skills to match the ever greater complexity of industrial organizations and technologies.

4 The Nature of Trade Unionism

I hesitate to add to the great volumes that have already been devoted to the trade union movement. It is really quite remarkable that such a bibliography should have been built up so rapidly. As part of the architecture of our national life, trade unions are relatively new and untried; nearly 2,000 years younger than the establishment of Christianity, 600 years younger than the universities, 200 years younger than modern science, and very much younger than industrialization itself. For those who regard the trade unions as old-fashioned, having lived beyond their usefulness, or an institution of the last century or the 1930s, it is right that they should understand that whatever is said about them, the unions are still young, still not certain of their role. Their power is still largely untried and their abilities are by no means at full stretch.

Yet this still does not answer the question: why the excitement? Why are the diligent social historians so eager to dissect and discover their role in the past? Why are the sad prophets so anxious to foretell their doom? Why the bitter critic denouncing their influence? Really it is not hard to uncover the reason. The trade union movement has always stood uncompromisingly on one particular side of the great social divide. It has remained on the side of the working people. The advocacy of Church and

university has been less certain, but for the trade union movement there has been only one goal and that is the championship
of ordinary working people. It is this that has made them a con-
tentious institution, and undammed the torrent of words and
opinions. For some they are cast in an heroic role as champions
of the fight for freedom and equality. Just as the ancient
Israelites bore with them into battle the Ark of the Covenant
that contained written proof of their birth-right and their
mission, so some have looked on the trade union movement as
the bearer of all true revolutionary values. For others, on the
other side of the old social divide, the unions are the usurpers of
order and rectitude, a Mafia plotting to subvert well-bred
society. For yet a third group, less concerned with social
divisions, the unions are looked upon, often with affection,
sometimes with exasperation, as a tough but slightly stupid cart-
horse, strong in the leg but a little weak in the head: very much
the image of David Low's cartoons.

Looking back through history, we can filter out the significant
events in the life of the trade union movement. With the benefit
of hindsight we can see quite clearly the inevitability of first the
development of trade unions, and then their acceptance. It is
easy now to identify the sometimes erratic, but nevertheless
unquestionable progress from the position of outlaws in an
early raw industrial society to that of a partnership in the drive
for national solvency and efficiency today. Yet for those who
manned the barricade, particularly in the early years, the final
national acceptance of the trade union movement was by no
means a foregone conclusion. These barricades were barricades
of incomprehension. They had to be this because conflict led to
conviction and conviction led to intolerance.

Even though today the trade unions are cemented into the
structure of our national life, the old arguments live on. Tired
spectres continue to haunt men's minds long beyond the point
when they have died away in real everyday life: the trade
unionist who cannot forget the 'thirties; the manager who lives

73

in the mental world of masters and men. Our opinions of trade unions one way or the other are difficult to budge because they are strong opinions. As a result, the mental lag between the reality of the position of the trade unions in society and people's thoughts on the subject has been a big one. If the historical development of the movement comes to be better understood there will be an opportunity to narrow this mental gap.

When one does look back a hundred and fifty years to the beginning of the combination of workmen in pursuit of their collective aims, one cannot but feel a certain irony. The attitude of the trade unionist towards the law has turned full cycle, from defiance to defence. For the early leaders their whole life was spent playing cat and mouse with the law. They were forced to be rebels and outlaws. Today, in place of sturdy defiance is equally sturdy defence of the law. Trade unions are now if not part of the Establishment then at least part of the established order. The law, apart from administering justice, undoubtedly preserves established order. When the legal position of the trade unionists is under fire, trade unionists will naturally enough wish to defend their hard-won position. For a place has indeed been won.

The turning point may well have been the General Strike of 1926, but certainly the position of the trade union movement in the national economy has completely changed during the past half-century. From being an organization in continuing and bitter strife within industry it has been transformed into the fourth estate of the realm. No government of any political colour would today fail to take the leaders of the trade unions into its confidence or seek the guidance and advice of the trade union movement on all matters which affect the economy and have an impact on the social changes and conditions of the people. This change did not come suddenly for as far back as 1932 the then National Government invited representatives of the General Council of the Trade Union Congress to attend the Ottawa Conference. Trade unionists are invited to serve on

74

innumerable public boards. A firm tradition has been established for the appointment of prominent trade unionists on the boards of the nationalized industries. The Bank of England has had at least one member of its Court drawn from this field since it was nationalized in 1946. The National Economic Development Council, which today perhaps represents the most powerful and influential planning body that the United Kingdom has ever had, is made up of the representatives of the General Council of the Trade Union Congress sitting, with the top-level representatives of British industry, alongside the economic Ministers in Government with the Prime Minister in the chair.

The desire of Government to control more effectively the economy so as to ensure a continuous steady growth meant a move towards a wages policy which implied some measure of control to prevent wage movements being inflationary. The positive action leading to the 'wage freeze' would have been quite impossible without the co-operation of the trade union movement. The agreement, therefore, of the trade unions and the employers' associations with the Government's incomes policy, which was recorded in the famous 'letter of intent', marks a new era of co-operation, the end of which cannot yet be clearly seen. There are and will be many difficulties of one kind and another before the perfect association can be said to have been achieved and the ideal relationships established between trade unions, employers' associations and governments, but despite the cynics, substantial progress has been made.

It is only necessary to look back over the history of the past hundred years to appreciate the metamorphosis that has occurred. Employers and management who decry the trade union movement and make it difficult to operate are making a great mistake and seriously misjudging the significance of its role: with all its imperfections it is here to stay, entrenched in the very vitals of industry and heart of Government.

The vital task of management and trade union leadership is to get right down to the rank and file the forward thinking now at the top leadership level. The pace towards progress of the trade union membership is determined by the slowest moving sectors, and there is no doubt that among the rank and file there are many hundreds of local leaders whose minds are still very much coloured and conditioned by the past. These men should not be condemned out of hand for their narrowness of view, their continuing suspicions of management objectives, and their easy willingness to be influenced by the demagogue and the trouble-making agitator. They are the product of an age that has passed but whose psychological impact still conditions the mind today. Wise management will recognize these facts of life and condition their own thought and efforts to help to speed up the change.

If management intends to do its human engineering correctly then it must first of all know something about the trade union movement in Britain. It is essential for management not only to know the organization as a structure but it must understand and look below the surface for its motivation.

The principal tasks of the trade union here, on the Continent, or in the United States are, first, to secure the best wages and conditions of service for its members and, second, to organize and strengthen its membership in order to improve its bargaining power. Its ultimate weapon is the withdrawal of labour to enforce its demands. At that point the similarity of the trade union movement in these three world sectors ceases.

In the United States the trade unions do not support any one particular party. They support either Democratic candidates or Republican candidates according to the pledges made on specific issues. On the Continent the unions are divided in their political allegiance and tend to be based either upon Marx's philosophy on the one hand or on the other on the Catholic Church. These create strains within the trade union movement even within the same industry, creating further problems for management in industrial relations. But in Britain the trade union movement massively supports the Labour Party, both financially and with service. Often men in management say to me, 'What a pity the trade unions are so political, it colours their whole attitude in industry.' This particular point of view is shared by a very large number of people indeed, and it is essential if management is going to make any headway at all in industrial relations to recognize why this is so and instead of wishing for a change to recognize that there is no likelihood in the foreseeable future of any change in these political associations. This is nowhere better explained for those who want greater knowledge or deeper understanding of the struggle for recognition by the trade unions, than in the history of the T.U.C., published to commemorate the centenary of the movement.* But for the purpose of this book let me try to paint the picture with a broad brush. This is essential if the reader is to understand the thinking behind the views and conclusions expressed in later chapters.

It has to be appreciated that the trade union in Britain is not a business organization designed to sell labour as a commodity, but is truly a movement that has grown through the years in accordance with its environment, so that to invite the trade unions to eschew politics is to ask them to abandon their genesis and historical past. Management need to know at least the bare bones of this background in order to understand the motivation lying behind a good deal of the thinking of the rank and file, which has its impact on local leadership and through them to national leadership of the trade unions.

The early days of the craft unions presented little or no difficulty in the relationship between master and servant. In the eighteenth and early nineteenth centuries, the craft guilds, forerunners of the trade unions, were set up almost like a secret society for the preservation of what were then the trade secrets or techniques. The apprentice was indentured to his master who worked alongside him, taught him the secrets of the craft,

* *A History of the T.U.C. 1868-1968: a Pictorial Survey of a Social Revolution* (T.U.C., 1968).

until in turn the young apprentice became his own master.

The revolt on the land, and the coming of the Industrial Revolution, changed all that. The story of the Tolpuddle Martyrs is too well known to relate here, but the fact that a number of farm labourers were banished as felons to Australia for the crime of leading agitation for a living wage for agricultural workers is still quite firmly fixed in the minds of the members of the Agricultural Workers' Union. Their annual pilgrimage to the village of Tolpuddle, where they have built workers' cottages as a memorial to the Tolpuddle Martyrs, each year commemorates the struggle of the early unionists.

This history does not, of course, affect the relationships between the leaders of the agricultural industry and the union today, but young people are still fired with the zeal of the early trade unionists, and what is called 'militant trade unionism' becomes the order of the day when industrial relations problems arise.

The Combination Act forced men to conspire in secret because it was unlawful, with heavy penalties, to meet openly. The political motivation was therefore strong for new legislation to permit trade union association. Gladstone felt these strong pressures and did just that. The Reform Bill of 1867 unleashed a new and energetic approach by the trade unions to ensure much wider and stronger development. By November of that year, with the Royal Assent hardly dry upon the Act of Parliament, the London Working Men's Association was formed, with one of its original objects being to 'produce the political enfranchisement of the workers and promote the social and general interest of the industrial classes'. The Trades Union Congress was formed in 1868 by 34 delegates representing 118,000 workers and in 1869 decided to appoint a Parliamentary Committee. The object again was to secure by political action that which had not been possible by industrial means.

Although this is a recital of happenings of a hundred years

back, the political roots of the trades union movement are deep and it is not surprising that political pressures are still a dominant factor in their affairs. By 1871 Gladstone produced a Trade Union Bill which, while it granted full and legal recognition to the trade unions, made legal industrial action very difficult indeed, if not impossible. The trade unions then made tremendous attempts to separate their status from the criminal classes, and finally political activity resulted in the Trade Union Act of 1871 and with it the Criminal Law Amendment Act.

Not many years had passed between the release of pent-up emotions by the Reform Act and further political action by the trade unions. This showed that the trade unions were as deeply political as they were industrial. Soon, however, the penalties of the Criminal Law Amendment Act were imposed, and perhaps the first occasion was the case of the Beckton gas stokers in 1872. In addition to convictions under the Master and Servant Act for the offence of striking, sentence of a year's imprisonment for the crime of conspiring to molest the company was imposed. Coalminers too were sentenced for crimes committed under this law during strikes. Indeed it was found to be almost impossible to call a strike without breaking the law, so that the only absolute sanction of the workers to withdraw their labour in defence of what they regarded as their just claims was denied them.

Thus the law, which had been made by their industrial masters, still stood in the way of trade union development. There was nothing else for it but to get people into Parliament who would change the law. The immediate years after 1871 saw the trade unions engaging in a nationwide campaign to secure the repeal of what they regarded as the obnoxious Criminal Law Amendment Act and also further amendments of the law relating to Master and Servant. In 1874 there came the General Election, and the first trade union Members of Parliament had arrived. Thomas Burt, a miner, represented Morpeth in Northumberland, and another miner, Alexander MacDonald, was returned at Stafford. Thirteen candidates had been put up by the Labour Representation Committee, which had become virtually a trade union body under William Allen, its President, an engineer, and Broadhurst, its Secretary, a stonemason.

The Labour Representation Committee, which was determined to put people supporting Labour into Parliament, was manifestly now run as a trade union pressure group. In 1885 the trade unions affiliated to the Trade Union Congress had about half a million members and by 1890 they had nearly 1,600,000. In 1893 the Independent Labour Party was founded and those mainly responsible were again the representatives of the workers. Famous names in the trade union movement were at the original meeting to form the I.L.P., and the trade union movement was from that moment firmly bound up in political action.

So from year to year right up to this present day the Labour Party has continued to be the child of the trade union movement. I do not mean to say of course that all trade unionists support the Labour Party or that even all the leaders of the trade union movement are vigorous supporters either, but it is the case that the trade union movement has provided the men and certainly the money for the Labour Party as we know it today.

The strange thing is that while trade unionists have been numbered among the leaders of the Labour Party, they have never yet produced a Labour Prime Minister. In these last years the trade unionists in the House of Commons, while considerable, have not been the majority on the Labour Party side. Nevertheless, they have been a very powerful influence in Government and out of it. As the years have gone by, however, the Trade Union Congress has come to be recognized by successive Governments as the body representing the trade union movement on matters of political as well as industrial content, and the trade union Member of Parliament is today becoming less and less of an influence. The leaders of the trade unions, mobilized in the T.U.C., have assumed all the authority that the trade union Members of Parliament formerly had. Indeed, the T.U.C. have tended more and more to be directly consulted by Governments and to make their representations directly to Government rather than through the trade union Members of Parliament, who may often in the House of Commons feel frustrated at this change in affairs. This by-passing has also had a profound effect upon the quality of the trade unionist in Parliament. Strong leadership tends to gravitate towards where the power lies, and for the trade unions it lies no longer solely in Parliament.

Nevertheless, there can be no doubt that the trade union movement still has its roots deep in politics. It is therefore no use employers today pining for a day when active trade unionists will cease to be political and support, in the main, the Labour Party.

The trade union movement today spends a good deal of its time pursuing social aims for the community as a whole in addition to the direct interests of its individual members. It has a deep collective sense of purpose for communal benefit and social change, and it is important for employers dealing with trade unions to understand that this is so. The communist influence in the trade union movement has, in fact, used this political basis to try to secure political objectives through industrial action. Since the war in particular there have been many cases of industrial disputes which had less to do with wages and conditions than the securing of communist political policies.

One should never forget, therefore, that within the trade union operating in industry or at the plant, action for political ends will form part and parcel of the leadership's thinking. In a free society there can be no objection to this: political activity will necessarily go hand-in-hand with trade unionism. Management should not jump too easily to the conclusion that active trade unionists are agitators whose only desire is to create disruption. Nevertheless, there are dangers and it is important that management should ensure that workers are aware of the facts of a situation and that no opportunity is given for the demagogue to twist the facts and make a trap for others.

With all this in mind, the whole question of communication and negotiation becomes more and more important. Where workers today have full access to all the information about their job, the company's objectives, and the possibilities of change, there is less likelihood of the real work of the trade union being thwarted for alien political purposes. Equally, the employer must make absolutely certain that he is not ascribing to base political motives, activities which are really the result of bad management or management which has not taken account of the changing conditions.

Today, men and women in industry are fully capable of understanding the facts of life if these facts are properly represented to them. In the main they have a very deep-rooted loyalty to their fellow workers, to their trade union and those who are politically conscious to their political faith. These are all, in fact, good attributes of an intelligent and civilized modern society. It is essential, therefore, that those in management should understand that these attributes are prevalent and that they are not to be discouraged but are, in fact, the product of an advanced and intelligent society.

It is not the task of management to try to wean away the loyalty of the trade unionist to his union or the active political unionist to his political party, but to recognize that in a free society a full rein must be given to individual feelings on these matters. At the place of employment, if the emphasis can be put upon the impact of a worker's efforts upon his own future and well-being and that of his fellow workers, the results in terms of greater efficiency will be a substantial reward for all the effort it requires. The trade union official today, whether a shop steward working at his trade, a branch secretary who is partly working at his trade but spending many hours, voluntarily in most cases, in the pursuit of his trade union activities, or a full-time officer looking after a very large number of men, carries a very heavy responsibility and often has to do it without proper services being available to him. Such men spend a tremendous amount of time, very often not because it is a professional job, as is the case of the full-time official, but because it is something in which they sincerely believe. It becomes a vocation and produces dedicated men.

The employer ought not to make the task of the trade union official more difficult but should go out of his way to make it easier. This won't buy the trade union official, in any shape or form, nor is it intended to, but if we are to get real co-operation between workers and management we must assist the trade union officer to do his job effectively and improve the efficiency with which he serves his members. An efficient trade union is not inimical to the interests of the employer or the nation. High earnings and a constant demand on the part of the mass of workers for a continuing higher standard of life are the essentials in a country of economic growth.

Co-operation between unions and management for mutual benefit depends a great deal upon the attitude and mental approach of the employer. The employer controls the administration and makes the decisions. Workers react to these decisions. It is in this field of the making of decisions that the greatest care should be taken to ensure that decisions should not come as a shock or surprise calling forth a reaction.

At one point in our history, and that a not far distant one, management were concerned only with the manual worker. It was the manual worker who made up the great trade unions. The miners, the dockers, the railwaymen—the 'Triple Alliance' which was smashed by the 1926 General Strike—constituted the great powerful trade union movement right up to 1939. The white-collar workers remained largely unorganized. The professional people like the teachers, the bank employees, the draughtsmen, and the like, eschewed industrial action and relied upon a benevolent management to provide pay and conditions that were tolerable. Now the mines, the docks, railways and agriculture employ fewer and fewer men. The membership of their unions declines. But there is a growing membership of the white-collar workers in unions, and with it a degree of militancy unthought of in pre-war years.

There are just over 11 million white-collar workers today in Britain; within a decade they will outnumber the manual workers. The growth of the new technological society will have changed completely the format of the trade union movement. It is extremely unlikely that the trade union movement will accept a situation of gradual decline by ignoring these changes in employment. It is more likely to go all out to organize the rapidly growing army of white-collar workers. With its great traditions and struggle for power it is most unlikely to fail to win over and organize this new rapidly growing army of workers who only a few decades ago were regarded as 'bosses' men'.

Employers should face these changes as the new facts of industrial life. To go through the same struggle as their forbears would be a tragic error of judgment. Better to welcome the change, prepare for it and accept that the new trade unionism will be different from the present and that it represents a new opportunity for industrial relations which could mark a new era in our industrial life.

If, however, the rise in the white-collar worker is met by the refusal of employers to recognize the unions of men's choice, then history could repeat itself to the grave detriment of the national economy. It is a mistake to believe that in a modern society the raison d'être for the existence of a trade union is merely to regulate wages and conditions. The union exists to discuss management decisions on all matters which affect or are likely to affect its members, and this does not leave much out. It has the right to question and to challenge; to consult and be consulted.

Man management is not the only problem that faces the business manager, but it is one that demands a very different approach from his relations with Government, customers, suppliers, shareholders and outside bodies. At the end of the day management have to look to the economic out-turn of the productive or service unit. The trade union has only a small or even no active place in many of the matters which concern management. It is, however, concerned with profitability and in this field it can aid very considerably. The modern trade union leader recognizes the importance of profits. His interest lies in ensuring that a fair share of the profits goes to his members. This is the new approach.

We shall not get the best out of our only real asset, man-power, if it is dissipated by a repetition of the struggle for recognition, which so disturbed relations between management and manual workers and from which we still suffer today. The white-collar worker will undoubtedly be organized and will certainly secure recognition for the purposes of genuine negotiations on all matters affecting his life at work. Employers who today, for a variety of reasons, are fighting a battle against recognition, are fighting a rearguard action which they will finally lose. A Canute approach to the rising tide of the new unionist will give the employer wet feet and the economy pneumonia. The nature of trade unionism is changing fast, and wise management will do all they can to hasten it. There is no need to teach the new union leadership that to stay in business means producing progressively at lower costs. Nor the fact that capital has to be borrowed if investment is to be sufficient to modernize and keep up with technical development. Nor are trade union leaders incapable of reading a balance sheet and making a shrewd assessment of that part of the profits which should go to labour. It is better that the arguments should be about these positive things than that industry should suffer internecine warfare because management feels they cannot share some of this decision-making with the representatives of the workers. The cash rewards that can come as a result of the co-operation of the new unionism with management will lead quickly to higher standards of living and an expanding economy free from punishing inflation. It will be more than a pity if the present opportunities are lost as a result of soured relations.

Wherever men are drawn together in groups, in whatever field, they will fight for what they regard as their interests. This spirit permeates all strata of life and social classes. It draws people together in a common interest in sports, pastimes, the Church, recreation, hobbies and all the strange and varied assortment of things people do in their lives. In work life the combination is stronger and more permanent. This is really the very nature of mankind since the beginning when combination and unity of interest was essential to keep alive. So it is today, and essentially that is the nature of trade unionism.

The costly errors of the past must not be repeated today. The growing numbers of craftsmen and technologists, without whom economic progress is impossible, need to be trained not only in their crafts and skills, but in the wider context of the business in which they are involved. Only then can they appreciate and understand the role that they need to play to secure improvements in their standards of living. At the same time the nature of trade unionism must be thoroughly understood and appreciated by the employer. Changes should be encouraged and welcomed. Resistance to this change can only result in industrial warfare which at most can but slow down the tide, but cannot hold it back. Meanwhile, while the battles rage, the progress of the economy is slowed and in the end the only victors are our foreign competitors, whose share of the world markets will continue to grow, while the share of the United Kingdom declines.

Industrial peace is an essential ingredient of a successful and financially viable Britain. It can only be secured if the trade union movement is not only recognized but welcomed and made a partner at all levels. High profitability is no longer sneezed at by the modern trade union leader. He knows that high profits and competitive prices give his membership exactly what they desire: security of employment, because the product has a sharp competitive edge and something really to bargain about in sharing the profits.

Progressive management should look upon trade unionism as an ally, and not as an obstacle. It should seek to bring it into a complete partnership with mutual interests in the financial success of the enterprise.

5 Consultation

The nineteenth century saw the development of the political democracy that is now part and parcel of our daily lives. The philosophy of 'one man, one vote' is today so much a matter of course that it is hard to believe that universal suffrage only finally came into being with votes for women at twenty-one years of age in 1928. The struggle, the sacrifice, the propaganda, the savageness of the argument is now forgotten by all except the historians. Indeed, universal suffrage has become so much a part of our way of life that we are in danger of imposing it upon every other emerging nation, whether they are ready for it or not. In many cases, because the ground has been insufficiently prepared, new emerging nations have decided that oppositions are a handicap to Government and disbanded them.

The twentieth century produced consultation in industry. It cannot yet be said to be wide enough or sufficient in depth throughout the whole of industry to have made the contribution that was confidently expected of it, but there can be no doubt that the contribution to the smoother and more intelligent operation of industry has been and is substantial. The seeds of industrial democracy have been well sown, but a fair amount of cultivation is required and still more growing time needed before the harvest can be reaped. Industrial democracy cannot be imposed, and will not grow overnight: it can only grow gradually with understanding, and the major responsibility for encouragement lies firmly with management. It is management who must finally make decisions, outside a syndicalist society, and management and management alone carries responsibility for the business and is answerable to the owners be they public or private.

Industrial democracy cannot parallel political democracy in giving everyone an equal voice in every decision, but it should mean that there is full and adequate consultation on all matters, and I must emphasize that none must be excluded. The channels of consultation must be adequate to ensure that matters for discussion flow up from workers to the most senior management. In the same way, policy decisions made at the top should flow down, with all the reasons and explanations that led to the decision, in such a way that changes in those policy decisions can be made if consultation shows weaknesses in the original decisions or that they could be further strengthened. The best, most constructive conclusions come from discussion, and the exchange of views between people with a common interest.

At whatever level in the structure of industry an individual may be, the opportunity to present a view should be there. Properly exercised, remarkable results can be achieved. Man is a gregarious animal and must not only live with others but identify himself with those around him. That is not to say he identifies himself with all the activities of all those in his environment, but only with those who have an identity of interest. That is why within a community there can exist a whole variety of activities, sports and pastimes, all well-organized and patronized without all the people in a community being interested in or wanting to do the same things. It is the difference between the herd instinct and the community interest.

Industry does in fact bring together all those who at a single moment of time have a particular single interest. Whether people are engaged in making motor-cars or teddy-bears, the identity of interest exists while they follow that particular occupation. When the individual changes his occupation his interest shifts, but a fresh identity of interest arises with those already at work in the particular occupation.

Industry, therefore, provides identity of interest but does not necessarily exploit that interest to the benefit of all concerned, i.e. the workers, the owners (public or private) and the consumers. Everyone is a consumer of other people's products and services and it is essential that the interest of the consumer should not be neglected by owner or worker. In many cases it would be true to say that competition takes care of the consumer; it would however be a great mistake to assume that competition exists everywhere, even though on the surface it may appear to be so. Monopolies, price rings, overt and covert, exist and even in the public services the protection of the consumer cannot apparently be left entirely to whatever consumers' councils may exist.

Consultation is not an end in itself but like most other actions it should have an aim, indeed a number of aims. There must, of course, be a main aim and this is fairly obvious and can be simply put. It is to maximize the use of the assets of the business by the most effective use of the manpower resources, both mental and physical. Fundamentally that is what consultation is about.

A good deal of academic nonsense is talked about consultation. Much hot air has been used to inflate speeches and articles about the aim of consultation being to make the worker 'feel he belongs' and that 'he is wanted', that he is 'part of a family'. Most workers reading or hearing these sentiments give a quiet smile. The truth is that the main aim of a worker in the present industrial society is to secure as big a pay-packet each week and as much leisure during the course of a year as possible. These are natural motives which match the desire of senior management to maximize the profits of the business, the wish of the shareholder to obtain the highest possible return upon his capital and the concern of the consumer to buy cheap.

Nineteenth-century capitalism regarded the aims of management and worker as completely incompatible. In order to provide goods and services cheaply, long hours of toil were regarded as essential. In my youth the forty-eight-hour week was the desirable objective of organized workers. In my father's youth a sixty-hour week was normal. Today the forty-hour week is fairly common for manual workers, with administrative workers round about thirty-five hours.

The struggle over the size of the pay-packet has been a long and bitter one and many of our industrial troubles today, in the older industries especially, stem from the bitterness of the past. The history of each trade union is a recital, page by page, of violent struggle and relations embittered in the fight by employers in the nineteenth century and the first three decades of the twentieth to keep wages down. They believed quite sincerely that higher wages meant lower profits. The mentality of the old mill-owners, who resisted the introduction of an Act of Parliament preventing children working in cotton mills, continued well into this century. High wages and ability to sell cheaply enough to keep and expand the market were incompatible, they said. All this has proved to be fallacious. High productivity can and does provide high wages, greater leisure and substantial fringe benefits without sacrificing profitability.

Joint consultation has played a major part in showing that this can be done, and in the main it has been management that has had to learn the lesson and, indeed, in many cases still has to do so. Unless management gives the lead these lessons cannot be generally applied. There will be many disappointments and failure will be registered from time to time on this problem and that. But patience, and determination and the will to make consultation work will bring astounding results, as all managements who have persevered over the years can testify. Joint consultation should not be regarded as a sop or palliative to the workers but as an essential part of running the business. It

91

provides an excellent training ground in the field of industrial relations, and it ensures that the one half of industry really does know how the other half lives and works.

Nevertheless, we must be realistic about the situation: I regard it as a fundamental error to suggest that we should stop talking about the two sides of industry because industry is a complete partnership and there should not be sides. This is an admirable sentiment but it lacks reality. There are undoubtedly two sides of industry: those who manage and those who are managed; those on one side who must accept the full responsibility for the proper government and control of industry and who in turn are strictly accountable to the owners, whether they be private shareholders or the State; and on the other side those who for a time, be it long or short, are subject to management. The first responsibility of the latter is to their wives and families, for their own pay and prospects of promotion, security of employment and possible outlets for employment for their sons and daughters. They have no responsibility for the conduct of the business as a whole and are only answerable to their immediate superior management for their own field of influence. They have a common interest with management in utilizing to the full the assets of the business, but only if that interest reveals itself in a steady improvement in their standards of living and security of employment, which in plain terms means cash to hand.

Workers are intelligent people who neither need nor want paternal patronage: they know full well that there are in fact conflicts between them and management, and regard oratorical statements from very senior management about the unity of industry with a fair degree of cynicism.

The fact that the unions in the main insist that joint consultation must not deal with wages and conditions is a clear indication that they certainly think in terms of two sides in industry. I do not deny that a complete unity of purpose in industry is highly desirable; indeed, the consultative process could be carried to the point when at each year-end the full financial results of the company could be discussed on the joint consultative agenda and agreement reached on the carve-up of the group profits, then the ultimate success of consultation would be achieved. I would indeed advocate ultimately a complete revelation of the financial out-turn in substantial detail and discussion and agreement about the amount to be ploughed back, reserves for the rainy day, self-financing, consumer pricing, return to the investors and the allocation for increased wages and/or improvements in fringe benefits. If and when this stage is reached then it might well be said there are not two sides in industry. Meanwhile, it is necessary to operate under the conditions as they are and maximize the use of joint consultation in industry until one day the next big step can be taken.

I have said that the principal aim of joint consultation should be to 'maximize the use of the assets of the business by the most effective use of the manpower resources' and I must repeat most emphatically that the worker will want to see just precisely what he is going to get out of it in terms of, first, cash in hand, and then better working conditions and all that goes with them. A good many by-products flow from that desire and a number of subsidiary aims emerge with which I will deal later.

First, it is essential for management to understand that joint consultation is not just a gimmick to make the worker feel happy but is an essential factor in proper human engineering, upon which the ultimate and continued success of the business depends. First-class effective consultation pays everyone hands down. Perhaps I may give an illustration from the coal industry to show this.

In an earlier chapter I indicated how great had been the impact of sustained and improved industrial relations upon the reduction of industrial disputes. Joint consultation has played its part in all this, but the real value of joint consultation has been in fields other than wage negotiations and the settling of piece rates, the major cause of disputes. I doubt very much if the immense changes that have occurred since 1957 in the mining industry could possibly have taken place with so little friction, without the efficient functioning of the machinery for consultation. Joint consultation is very real in the coal-mining industry, every pit having its own consultative committee, meeting regularly with a substantial agenda from which nothing is barred except matters which fall within the scope of the conciliation machinery. The men's representatives are drawn from every activity in the mine and the senior management, headed by the colliery manager, who chairs the committee, are also there so that every aspect of activity about the pit lies within the personal knowledge and responsibility of someone present. At the pit level, all matters affecting its working and operation as an individual unit can be dealt with in detail. Some matters which are of general interest to a wider group of collieries in an area are referred to an area consultative committee upon which sit the area officials of the unions and the area management. In these meetings all matters of common concern to all pits in the area are dealt with and there is little spill-over into problems of a national character. Should any of these be a question with national implications then there is a coal industry National Consultative Committee which deals exclusively with matters affecting the industry as a whole. The Chairman of the National Coal Board occupies the chair at these meetings and the whole of the activities and forward thinking of the Board are frankly disclosed and debated. Financial and business objectives, profitability and marketing, technical research and development projects are discussed in great detail. Everything, in fact, about the Board's activities, and in particular new policies to be introduced, is considered and explanations given in detail. From this meeting a clear and precise record goes to all the other consultative committees so that they are kept fully informed of what is being considered at national level.

What has been the impact of this joint consultation on the fortunes of the coal-mining industry?

I suppose one would point first to the complete metamorphosis of the industry from winning coal with a pick and shovel to virtually complete mechanization with high horse-power machines, remote-control techniques and other developments which have made the United Kingdom technically the foremost mining industry in the world. Incidentally, this has meant millions of pounds' worth of mining equipment manufactured in this country and exported to Europe and Japan, Australia and America.

By the year 1957 the coal industry was losing its monopoly as the energy supplier for the country. It faced a hard competitive battle with the new fuels: oil, nuclear power and, away on the horizon, natural gas. Gone was the exhortation by Government to produce coal, as much as possible without regard to price. In its place was the grim realization that coal in the future would only have a place if the price was competitive.

This meant that the evolution from pick and shovel to full mechanization had to proceed at top speed. At the end of 1957 only 26 per cent of coal mined was power-loaded, that is to say, cut and loaded on to the conveyor by machine. By 1969 it had reached 93 per cent.

No one, except those in mining, could possibly know what that meant in effort, strain and organization. Literally thousands of men had to be trained to handle enormous new complicated machines and their ancillary equipment. The planned maintenance of all this and the training of the craftsmen and others to deal with a revolution in mining techniques was so great that even the most optimistic were doubtful of success. Nevertheless it was accomplished, and with some amazing results. But the important thing to appreciate and realize is that this fantastic achievement could not possibly have been accomplished without the co-operation of the trade unions and the work of the consultative committees.

At the same time as it was tackling these tasks of training, installing heavy, awkward and powerful machines below ground, devising new techniques of mining operations to match the capabilities of the new machines demanded, the industry was also engaged in bringing down its capacity by the closure of large numbers of pits and transferring men at an unprecedented speed. No operation of this size and kind has ever been attempted to my knowledge anywhere in the world, and certainly has never before been carried out with such success. Perhaps it is best summed up in these few figures.

During the ten years 1959 to 1968, 506 pits were closed affecting the employment of 166,000 men, and 141,000 were transferred to other currently operating pits. Despite this vast movement face productivity rose by 77 per cent, overall productivity by 58 per cent, and there were virtually no industrial disputes arising from this cause.

In April 1962 a scheme was started to provide for the transfer of men and their families to other coalfields many miles from their old homes. Since that time, by 1969 over 10,000 men and their families have moved. Only the proper use of consultative machinery enabled these things to be done smoothly and easily. In my view it represents one of the finest examples of the value of adequate and full consultation.

I mention this because it was a great test of the principle of the consultative machinery which, although imposed as a legal requirement upon the industry by statute, has been evolved within the industry in a form best suited to the organization and the circumstances of coal mining.

Public enterprises all have a statutory obligation to provide for joint consultation, but the experience in the coal industry through the years has been so beneficial that even if it were not provided for by Act of Parliament there would certainly be no desire on either side to weaken or disband the machinery.

This is not to say that the consultative machinery produces 100 per cent of its potential: no one would want to make that claim. Consultation is, however, a growing thing and like a plant it has to be cared for, cultivated and fertilized so that one day its roots will be embedded firmly enough to find its own sustenance and continued sturdy growth.

Joint consultation is not new. Some firms have been practising it for fifty years or more. It naturally emerged from the pressure of the trade unions to extend their operations beyond the mere negotiations of wages to the wider applications of communal approach to the working environment of their members. There was the obvious need also to have the opportunity of joint discussion of local and national problems. The essential difference between negotiation and consultation is that negotiation is an argument in which both sides set out to succeed in establishing their point of view while consultation is designed as a discussion to establish the facts and arrive objectively at the truth of a situation and thus the logical solution to the problem.

The First World War gave a boost to joint consultation when the Government consulted the trade unions not just on wages and conditions but on ways and means of increasing productivity as a major contribution to the war effort.

The Whitley Committee set up in 1916 gave an impetus to joint consultation in an endeavour to improve the relationship between management and work-people, and there is plenty of practical evidence available to show that consultation in a number of companies has worked effectively in improving relationships and co-operation. Despite this long period of gestation, the introduction of consultative machinery has been extremely slow. The Ministry of Labour did what they described as a rough and ready survey in 1957 and concluded that about 65 per cent of firms in private manufacturing, employing upwards of 500 people, have no consultative machinery. There may be many reasons for this, but whatever they may be I believe these firms lack a vital piece of machinery to make their operations more efficient. It is of course pointless to install consultative machinery unless like any other machine it is fully understood and is operated correctly. Unless the work of the consultative committee is made interesting, and the views of the workers' representatives are really taken fully into account before decisions are made, then the system fails. It is not a bit of use having consultative machinery which seems to exist solely for the dissemination of management decisions. The initiative for making consultation work effectively must lie with management and its readiness to discuss important issues such as redundancy, changes in methods of work and a willingness to explain and if necessary defend managerial views, policy and decisions.

The aim of joint consultation is, clearly, to inform and in return be informed. The essence of the exercise is to enable both the work-people and management to approach their respective tasks with an intelligent appreciation of all the factors involved in working together to earn a living. No problem that is man-made is incapable of solution by man. But the solution to problems and a proper understanding can often come only from frank and objective discussion. Very often the solution to a problem is not immediately apparent, but it is quite surprising how eventually an answer becomes clear as discussion takes place. It is indeed doubtful if ever at any time in history a single individual has, out of his own mental resources, found the final answer to a major problem. It is by talking and exchanging views that a solution is finally sparked off in someone's mind.

The aims of joint consultation are so valuable if realized that, despite the many problems that consultation itself produces, no employer can afford not to encourage it and by example and leadership make joint consultation work.

There can be no doubt that joint consultation must show concrete results if the interest of the workers is to be sustained. Equally, it should be possible to discuss any matter from the canteen meals and service to the balance sheet and everything in between. Certainly it should enable workers to channel their discontents and air the day-to-day grievances which are bound to arise. Management should never baulk at frequent meetings of the consultative committees: grievances that can fester and build up into something really serious can be dealt with in infancy with the right type of consultative machinery. It is extraordinary but true that there are more industrial disputes over working conditions than over wages. The grievance that is not handled at source becomes a rallying point for the agitator who prefers trouble to peace in industry. No one ever built a steam engine without a safety valve or an electric motor without a cut-out to meet the danger of overload. The case for consultative machinery is that it is the opportunity for intelligent people to be able to express dissatisfaction and calmly discuss it. It may well be that the worker will tend to have more grievances to air than management. Nevertheless, management too will have grievances and they should not hesitate to voice these through the consultative committee. Management will often be surprised that what they imagine is self-evident is not as plain as all that to the worker, and a discussion upon a management grievance may often bring surprising results of co-operation and practical solutions to problems from the workers' point of view.

It is essential that discussion of welfare and amenities should find a forum in joint consultation. A man spends nearly a third of his life at work. What happens there in terms of personal welfare and the amenities with which he is surrounded is important. If the factory is going to be repainted, let the consultative committee have the chance of expressing a view about the colour. If a new canteen is to be provided, let the consultative committee see the proposals, examine the plans and suggest the kind of equipment to be provided down to the merest detail. When the new canteen is finished and opened for use there will be as many stout defences of it against the critics on the workers' side as on the management. It will be their canteen, they will have had an equal say with management in its provision. It is an important amenity that they have to live with every day of their lives. Such a facility has a greater impact upon the worker than the management.

No matter which relates to the man's working environment should be regarded as trivial because it does not directly deal with productivity or profits. A man's environment is important to his attitude of mind to his work. All amenities are important —however small they may appear to management.

The same can be said of welfare. All man's welfare cannot be dealt with on a community basis, but there is a great deal that can. There is much that could be done in industry which is not done, and joint consultation provides the right avenue of approach for improving and extending existing welfare facilities. The provision of welfare in various parts of industry is quite extensive but it cannot be said to be intensive.

The earliest forms of joint consultation grew around the provision of amenities and welfare and it was not for nothing that this was so. These subjects still remain important and basically personal and while with the passing of the years ideas and requirements change, fundamentally they are still the foundation upon which joint consultation rests. They remain the roots and it is of little use expecting to gather big apples off the boughs if the roots are in any way neglected. The problems of the workers need to be attended to before they can possibly be expected to give adequate consideration to the problems of management.

An individual's job becomes more interesting when he is made aware of how his particular task, which may not be very interesting in itself, fits into the whole. Joint consultation provides the means of enabling the worker to see the whole of the production problems and the ramifications of the industry. At the end of the day the whole point about production is to sell the product, at home or abroad or both. If the goods produced do not give user or consumer satisfaction then sales inevitably fall, with the resultant reduction in output and the prospect of reductions in the payroll. Job insecurity is certainly not what the worker wants and joint consultation can indicate immediately the relationship of production to sales. The experience of the man on the job is invaluable and the collective advice can do much to improve either the quality of the product itself or the method of manufacture. This combined knowledge, if brought to bear on the problems of selling and merchandising, can have a considerable effect on the progressive growth of the company or industry. The pooling of all these factors and the careful selection of items for detailed examination is a most useful function of joint consultation. The important result which emerges is the healthy all-round interest in the affairs of the company, and as nothing succeeds like success, enthusiasm tends to grow rapidly as mounting commercial success follows.

Unless there is a substantial degree of understanding and confidence between management and worker it will be well-nigh impossible to exploit to the full the very rapid changes in techniques already taking place in industry and in prospect. There has been nothing in our industrial history to compare with the speed of change that has now to be faced. The Industrial Revolution of the early part of the last century changed the lives of a whole population, it is true, but over a fairly long period of years. The Cybernetic Revolution which has now begun is likely to grow at an extraordinarily fast rate. So far the new techniques have largely come from the space research programmes and defence generally: computerization, automation, printed circuits and ultra-fine precision engineering to name but a few. Quite soon the lessons to be learned from these new developments will become incorporated to a far greater extent in our industrial life. The nation which seizes these new opportunities first and successfully applies them to industry and commerce will be a world leader with the high standards of living that go with that position.

Quite soon now the computer will be within the price and

size range of literally thousands of business organizations which so far, either because of size or cost or perhaps both, have been unable to take advantage of this newest weapon in the industrial and commercial armoury. The speed by which the computer itself has moved in its development is some indication of what effect it in turn will have upon the speed of change in our industrial life. It might be as well to recall here that the first electronic computer in the world was built at Manchester University during the 1940s. Subsequently, computers were built at Cambridge University and the National Physical Laboratory and by 1951 Ferranti had made one for commercial sale. In twenty-five years the computer has come from design to commercial practice over a growing but limited field. In the next twenty-five years it will make a momentous impact on the working lives of people, no less upon management than upon workers.

Without adequate joint consultation the introduction of these new techniques could go off at half cock. If by the use of adequate joint consultation the veil of mystery is swept away from these new techniques and the full value exploited rapidly, the impact on the lives of the people and upon the nation for good would be unimaginable.

The very action of joint consultation itself stimulates progressive thought and breeds efficiency. It is not, however, something that can be imposed: it must of itself come from discussion and consultation. Where the trade union is already established, the vehicle for discussion is there and, in the main, provided that the joint consultative committees keep off matters of wage negotiations, then the trade unions, which are committed to the principle of joint consultation, are co-operative and willing to help in the formation of the actual consultative machinery. Management should beware of preparing a cut-and-dried scheme and virtually imposing it, however good and pure their motives might be. Certainly it would be up to the management to prepare the basis of a scheme for joint consultation, but only as an aid for discussion so that the eventual machinery finally adopted is the outcome of joint consultation itself.

The kind of joint consultation will differ from firm to firm and industry to industry. Meanwhile, it is important to empha-size that in entering into joint consultation, management are voluntarily relinquishing their full managerial authority, and it is of little use management entering into this field, or expecting the best out of joint consultation if they have already entered it, unless they recognize this essential fact. Joint consultation as a pretence or as a sop to workers 'to keep them quiet' will assuredly fail. Joint consultation must mean that action arises out of decisions arrived at by consultation and the actions must be seen to be as a result of consultation.

It must mean, too, that management must be ready to con-cede changes arrived at by consultation and be ready to accept that, in expressing his views in joint consultation, the worker is not interfering with management but expressing a point of view which requires discussion and explanation. Joint con-sultation will not work, will not produce worthwhile results, no matter how genuine the desire of the employer and the trade union leadership to ensure its success, unless senior manage-ment on the one hand and the trade union leadership on the other educate and train their representatives at lower levels in the skills and techniques of joint consultation. It is no use throwing men and management into joint consultation at the deep end before they can swim. Adequate training in this field as in all others is essential for success. But despite all the care and preparation success in joint consultation does not come easily. Above all it needs patience, for only with the passage of time and practical experience can the necessary confidence emerge that finally gets the best from joint consultation. What-ever the difficulties and disappointments, there can be no doubts whatsoever that thousands of days are being lost in industrial disputes every year because of the failure of adequate joint consultation, and in so many cases the complete absence of it.

Human engineering cannot possibly succeed unless the tools are complete and available, and joint consultation is one of the most valuable of these.

6 Communications

The mechanics of communications have developed rapidly in recent years, and nobody now takes much notice when it is announced that the telecast of a boxing match in America is being transmitted to us in Britain through a satellite in outer space. We accept that science has made such progress and are content to accept the benefits as they come: but communications is an art as well as a science in the sense that what people wish to know is still a matter of choice.

Most people like to be aware of what is going on around them. It is often the only method they have for relating their activities to those of other people; and everyone possesses what some would describe as a thirst for knowledge, others as a natural curiosity.

How do we get the information we want? what do we do with it when we have it? and how do we react when we suspect that we are not getting adequate supplies? These are all matters of great importance to us in our work as well as in our private encounters.

We have gone a long way in the development of the means of communications but we still have some lessons to learn about how to make use of them.

The speed at which we all respond to new information and absorb it, and the manner in which different people react to the stimulus it brings, are well worth the study of everyone with any degree of managerial responsibility.

In some cases a message can bring an impact which spells out an immediate lesson, or a number of lessons; in others the message might involve the sowing of a seed in people's minds which will take time to germinate and eventually come to flower.

Both examples could be demonstrated by a well-known after-dinner story about post-war rehabilitation and how its social and economic implications were brought home to two individuals in a short sharp encounter. A man who had recently returned from serving abroad walked down the steps of a London hotel and placed what he thought was an appropriate coin in the hands of the commissionaire who had hailed his taxi.

The commissionaire, who had grown used to tips which were highly inflationary by pre-war standards, regarded the coin as it lay in the palm of his hand and asked, 'Can you spare it, sir?' The giver was a just man who liked to make fair decisions but he was no slouch when it came to making up his mind when he appeared to have all the available facts. He considered the problem too. 'No,' he replied. 'On second thoughts I can't.' And he took the coin and put it back into his pocket.

There is an obvious lesson in communication here: the speed of the message was sharp, and its effect peremptory. And it affected both men equally. One probably concluded that tips were going to be lower in future, while the other must have been starting to deliberate on whether or not to increase his rate of tipping.

It is appropriate to quote a story drawn from more than twenty years ago because it was in the post-war period, when men's minds were very open to prospects of change, that the demand for better communications really began to grow. People had become used to the idea of being 'put in the picture'. It had been necessary if a maximum war effort was to be achieved. Something which in wartime was thought to be rather novel was coming to be taken for granted. This was in very sharp contrast to the attitudes prevailing in the First World

War, when paternalism was the order of the day and men expected to do as they were told without any explanation.

The need for good communications is now becoming more
clearly understood. It takes place between people who think,
feel and behave. It is a two-way traffic. And it is a process
which must be continuous. This is an important aspect of the
subject because social habits are developing and changing
rapidly and the good communicator, like the good car driver,
must always be trying to read the road ahead.

Telling people what they need to know, while accepted as a
necessary function in industrial relationships, has developed a
long way since the 'put 'em in the picture' stage. This was an
excellent and necessary wartime expedient and was regarded
as such at the time by many people in management: but it
meant very little more than developing the negative into a
positive print. It must, of course, be remembered that everyone
was at that time agreed on what the final objective ought to be,
and it is relatively easy to unite people of all classes against a
common danger. It is not, however, quite so easy to obtain
anything like the same degree of accord with the problems
likely to be met in an industrial society.

The two-way process also is something which must be understood if it is not to fall into the category of a meaningless cliché.
Anyone who has spent a holiday abroad knows something of the
difficulties of translation. There are some things that can be
registered quite as well in sign language as they can in any other,
but customs and habits of mind which are ingrained take longer
to understand. There is therefore a twofold problem in two-way
traffic, and those responsible must be sure that anything that
has to be communicated must be couched in language which will
be comprehended as easily by the receiver as by the sender.

This sort of understanding must be carried through right
down the line of management from the top to the bottom. It is
axiomatic that junior management, as well as the workers in an
industry, must be kept fully informed if they are to give of their

best. The board of directors and their senior management have to have all the economic facts of their business at their fingertips if they are to formulate policy, but whatever they decide stands a decreasing chance of becoming effective if there is a lack of information lower down the line. So the wise employer explains the reasons for certain decisions if he expects to get an intelligent response from the worker and his trade union representative.

So much for theory. There are, however, those who put obstacles in the way of good communications. This may be because of an over-zealousness about what must be regarded as confidential information, or a belief that information should be kept to a close circle. Such an attitude is only too general and causes a great deal of harm. People are naturally curious and become suspicious and angry if they feel that they are being given a censored version of the facts. I am convinced that a great deal of time and money is wasted and decisions delayed by otherwise well-meaning people who put up barriers when none should be there, by a failure to release essential facts.

A weak point in the chain can be the failure of management to provide shop stewards and the local officials of unions representing those working in their factories and workshops with the necessary facilities to ensure adequate communication between the local leadership of the union and the rank and file members. The employer who fails to welcome the union as a channel of information is very definitely injuring the prospects of his company and himself as an individual. He is inviting a lack of confidence in all the information he shares with his employees through other channels, which I shall discuss later in this chapter. This kind of employer is creating the suspicion that his facts will not stand up to careful examination by the union's representatives and the members they represent.

No employer should attempt to by-pass the union as a channel of communication. To do so is to engender ill-will and resentment on the part of local union leadership. It is, however, true to say that the facilities generally available to local trade union leaders for the purpose of passing on information are very limited. All too many employers tend to take the view that this inadequacy is none of their business. I cannot urge too strongly that this is a mistaken view. Where it is evident that such facilities are inadequate, management would be well advised to improve them and see that they are working properly. They can do so without seeking in any way to interfere with union organization.

Policies within a union, whether at branch or national level, are made in the opposite way to policy decisions made by management. In management, policy decisions necessarily are made autocratically at the top of the pyramid, the subsequent information flowing down to the base. In the trade union movement the reverse takes place: the broad base of the rank and file membership put pressure upon their leaders and induce them to produce the policy which the executive of the union has democratically to carry out. It is therefore highly desirable, indeed just as essential, though more difficult, as it is in the case of management, for the rank and file to be well informed. Because of the poor arrangements made for meetings and in many cases the open hostility to the provision of such facilities by management, the rank and file in many workshops and factories are often inadequately informed and this can lead to all sorts of trouble.

The first priority, therefore, in the field of communication is for management to ascertain what the facilities are for contact between local trade union leadership and their members, and to take the initiative, in co-operation with the union branch, in establishing or improving them when they are not good enough. Employers should positively provide a place for properly constituted meetings on the firm's premises, assistance in the duplication and circulation of documentary information, use of telephones and somewhere for members with a grievance to go when they wish to consult shop stewards. There are many other requirements which individual examination would reveal. If the work of communication is to be effective, it must be encouraged to take place efficiently in suitable circumstances, rather than in the hole-in-the-corner way which is only too common.

It is extraordinarily difficult to get union members to attend branch meetings when these are held away from the place of employment, and not too easy even when they are held there. But the branch is the business unit of the workers' union and the branch is better able to play a part in the determination of policy if it is reasonably supported and the meetings held in circumstances which provide for convenience rather than inconvenience. Branches based on the place of work are advantageous to the union, and to its membership; and because a branch of a union based on the workplace will in the main be dealing with the problem of the work and the working environment, it serves the industry as well.

Good communications can only be successful where the organization is well and clearly defined. A vast amount of time in any organization is taken up with transmitting and receiving information, ideas and opinions and issuing or receiving orders and instructions. All information must be accurate and relevant and instructions clear and unambiguous. There should be no possibility of misunderstanding, and clarity in both writing and speaking is essential if this is to be avoided. It is also important that leap-frogging of any particular unit or class of worker does not take place.

One of the great mistakes frequently made in industrial relations is to overlook the importance of junior management, especially men in the foreman group. The wheels of industry can never turn efficiently if foremen are not kept fully aware of the group objective. They should never have to learn of changes from their subordinates, even though the subordinate is a trade union shop steward. Managers often boast that their office doors are open to everyone with a problem; this is a mistaken attitude. Any manager who seeks to solve the problems of an individual, other than a personal domestic problem, by making a settlement without reference to the individual's supervisor, or to whatever level of junior management may be appropriate, is, in effect, acting in a way prejudicial to effective management and the managerial structure. The importance of the foreman and junior management levels should never be overlooked in the system of communication.

The employer has a prime responsibility to inform and he must be sure that all levels of management thoroughly understand the policy and are able, through the opportunity of prior consultation, to support it. One should never permit a situation in which the junior management is merely being used as a post office to convey pre-determined decisions. They should be in the position to relate company policy to the men in their charge and be able to do it intelligently and answer questions about particular matters with which the men are concerned. In most factories the end-product is produced by a number of working groups, and meetings of small groups usually provide a more effective means of communication than a mass meeting composed of many groups. It is here that the junior management can play a very lively and important part. However, they must be thoroughly informed before they can play their part effectively and it is the task of senior management to ensure that this happens.

There are many fields to cover and many different methods of communication can be applied. I have already discussed the importance of joint consultative machinery, which provides a forum not only for discussion but also for information about health, safety, welfare, training, productivity, new techniques and new machinery.

The basic need is for managerial decisions and information to be explained directly to work-people by the representative of management who is responsible for their work. In this, of course, they will need additional aids. While personal conversation is the best method of communication it has necessarily to be aided by the printed word. No matter how advanced, how complex each industry becomes in the space age, this pressing problem of keeping people informed has to be solved. The brightest ideas, the most progressive policies and indeed the greatest goodwill are doomed to failure unless people know about them. They have to be explained and widely understood. The printed word is an essential element in this.

There are many factors that militate against good communications but size and location stand out as two very important ones. It is simple to keep in touch with fifty people in a small workshop, more difficult in a factory of 550, and much more difficult in an industry like mining where nearly half a million people are involved. It is easy to recognize whether good communications are at work in a single factory, not so easy when workers are spread over a dozen or more plants scattered around the country.

The network of industrial newspapers and magazines is extremely important in helping to knit together scattered elements of industry. The choice of magazine or newspaper depends upon factors which can only be judged in relation to the particular circumstances of the industry concerned. I personally prefer the industrial newspaper, which can be printed so much more quickly than the magazine that it is possible to get the very latest news and information into it before publication. The newspaper style is more attractive to the average reader, provided it is written by professional journalists and presented in the right way. It is very important, however, that it should not be a 'boss's newspaper'. The industrial newspaper should be bright and lively, giving full coverage to views of union leaders and including a correspondence column that is prepared to print critical as well as appreciative letters.

Because of the huge payroll in the mining industry, the Coal Board's own industrial newspaper, which is printed monthly, has seventeen editions each of eighteen pages. It has a circulation of more than 200,000 copies a month, which means nearly one in two mineworkers buy it at 3d. a time. An industrial newspaper, however, does not need to have such a large circulation to be a good publication.

The industrial newspaper, as I have described it, is preferable to the house magazine: some of these journals have a pretentious 'glossy' appearance which combined with a layout like a stamp album, with deadpan faces staring out at the reader, and the chairman's annual report to the shareholders, or his Christmas message taking obvious pride of place, are not likely to have any impact, save the wrong one, on the reader. Too much space is often devoted to pictures and descriptions of retirement presentations and weddings of people unknown to the general body of readers, and too little space given to bread-and-butter topics such as wages, working hours and conditions of work.

The industrial newspaper has a completely different approach. It covers a much wider field of reader interest, and being written, as it should be, by professional journalists conveys information by a method which has the widest possible acceptance. I would emphasize again that the editing and writing of house journals and industrial newspapers is not a job for the amateur. Journalism is a profession and neither the house journal nor the industrial newspaper will be a success if it is not produced by an expert in his craft.

Most firms of any size need to use the printed word to reinforce other forms of communication. Many already use the monthly periodical and by no means all of them are bad. But they all need to keep in mind that to be acceptable they must entertain as well as inform and they would do well to avoid the dictum of Oliver Cromwell who thought that the public should have 'not what they want but what is good for them'.

One of the things that sometimes gives me cause for concern when I visit a factory is the condition of the notices on bulletin boards. There is nothing more depressing than some of the bulletin boards one sees from time to time. A single drawing-pin in the centre of a foolscap notice, turning the whole board into a series of paper tubes looking more like organ pipes, or a depressing exhibit of pop art. Some have old notices, long out of date. Others have new notices pinned on top of the old ones; and the whole effect is sad and lifeless. However, properly sited, well designed and efficiently maintained bulletin boards can be of great help and importance in the flow of information. But if good use is not made of the bulletin board it is better to scrap it.

The siting of notice boards is also very important indeed, and as they cost money and have a purpose to fulfil the sites for them should be chosen with great care. They are a comparatively cheap and effective way of getting information to a large number of people in a comparatively short time. But they need to be carefully watched to ensure that the message they bear does not outlive its function and stay on the board a day longer than is necessary. Constant notice-board changes, with information of an interesting nature, will create an inquisitiveness amongst work-people and encourage them to 'see what's on the notice board'. It is sensible too to have separate notice boards for specific purposes. It is, for example, a mistake to mix up company notices, sports and social activities, and trade union notices indiscriminately on the same board. A much better plan is to have separate boards for each.

One should not overlook the more modern methods of communication where the circumstances warrant it. Closed-circuit television can play a very important part in communications. I once addressed an audience of British scientists and fuel experts about the progress being made in modern mining. Sitting in the comfort of a Cambridge cinema, they saw on the screen a direct transmission from a Lancashire colliery at work. Just by pushing a button I was able to stop and start a coal conveyor below ground at that colliery 170 miles away, and everyone in the audience could see it all happening. You seldom get more effective communications than that. Closed-circuit television is in fact used daily at the pits for communication on matters of safety as well as part of the technique of control.

Another medium of communication which is becoming increasingly widespread is the use of film. This again is an established method of reaching our consciousness and a most effective one too because it makes an all-consuming claim on our eyes and ears. The spoken word can be interrupted, and the written word cannot always hold the reader, but once in the cinema our attention is held. The art of the documentary film was conceived in this country and its expertise has been employed widely both for education and training. It is possible, for example, to do more to prevent accidents in workshops, factories and mines by a film on safety than by almost any other method. More and more the film is being used in training, for instruction in the use of new machines, and latterly for indicating the marketing problems of a company, and the importance of quality and reliability.

It is essential that the man on the shop floor should understand the impact that the sales of the finished product can have on his salary and continuity of employment. Care in production has a vital part to play in his welfare, and there would be less shoddy workmanship if more individual workers were aware of the effect of the actual execution of their work on sales, both at home and abroad, of the finished product.

Many of our excellent documentary film makers have mastered the art of using work-people as leading actors in many kinds of industrial films, and the sense of involvement that this brings can be beneficial to the organization concerned. It is natural for the worker to adopt a cynical attitude towards exhortations from his employer, but appeals that may be rejected in other media may have a significant impact if translated into film, using the technique of portraying men themselves at work: this can bring out a man's pride in the job in a

115

way that no amount of exhortation can ever hope to do. And films employing these techniques are among the most enjoyable to watch. Once again, however, this is a job for experts, as anyone who has had to suffer the amateur versions will be only too glad to testify.

It has been said that the world can be divided between two sorts of people: those who want to read about others; and those who don't want to read about themselves. This may be based on the theory that what you read about others is interesting, while what you read about yourself is wrong—or exaggerated to say the least.

It would be a great pity if everyone took the latter view and attempted to by-pass or otherwise ignore what is traditionally the most widely accepted channel of information in our society. Good journalists go to a great deal of trouble to establish the essential facts of any story they are writing. It is better to help them get their facts right rather than risk being mis-reported merely by being unhelpful. It is also desirable for everyone in management to learn something about the ways of a medium in which, for example, many trade unionists are more adept than employers. This does not come easily to everyone and there are, as in all human relationships, traps for the pompous and pitfalls for the devious, but a point of view, or a statement of fact, clearly put will always do more good than harm for the organization in question.

The kind of personality that an organization wants to project is self-evidently a matter of interest and concern to those who are members of it at whatever level of employment they happen to be, and there is an obvious need for every major intention affecting an organization to be known to everyone on its staff. It has been said that a ticket collector cannot relate himself to the aims of the transport company he works for except in the efficient collection of tickets—which to him might mean an end in itself. This is an unimaginative view and its limitations can often be exposed by looking more closely at the personality of the man away from his work. He may be a quiet chap who pursues his hobbies and takes no active interest in the world around him. But he may be, and often is, a citizen who, as a trade unionist or a borough or city councillor, takes not only an interest, but sometimes has a considerable say, in matters relating to his work and indeed to the fortunes of his employers also.

An organization's relationships, through individuals, with the world outside the mine or factory are, therefore, matters of importance. There is nowadays a much more general interest in industry than in the pre-war years, and newspapers, television and radio are all anxious to portray people in relation to their work.

Society is becoming increasingly complex and many people in management tend to become the slaves of their own disciplines. This in turn leads them into an approach to their own knowledge which is more subjective than objective and makes the task of interpretation more difficult to undertake. It is, however, a problem which must be tackled and it is noticeable that many of the top men in their relative fields can relate the most abstruse subjects in comparatively simple terms.

I am not suggesting that every subject can be simplified down to the lowest level of acceptance, but it is obviously necessary to keep the door of information open. There are always many people pressing against it and wanting to come in. To deny them entry must always be considered a backward step.

An understanding of how to communicate is therefore an integral part of human engineering. Wherever there is waste or inefficiency, where assets or human resources are not fully used, there is also a lack of knowledge and a job for the communicator.

It is, I repeat, a continuous task. We live in an age of change, and there is greater movement of personnel at all levels both within and between industries now than at any time in our history.

The irrigation channels of knowledge must be kept clear and in good shape if the flow of information and ideas is to be unimpeded. I have always believed in the power of good communications and that training in this important subject should form part of the education of managers at all levels.

Communications within industry means much more than the dissemination of information from the top down. Communications need to be adequate to ensure that the message, the warning, etc., can come from the bottom upwards. In the previous chapter on consultation, I have said a good deal about this already. It is as well to emphasize again, however, that communications must operate upwards and sideways as well. Indeed lateral communications in particular, especially in large industry, require much more serious consideration than they are often given. Failure to have effective lateral communications can have disastrous effects.

In any firm of size, 'departmentalism' is inevitable and decision-making and directives and instructions down departmental channels are unavoidable. What is avoidable, however, is a situation in which the right hand is unaware of what the left hand is doing. The utmost care needs to be exercised to make absolutely sure that the functionalism of the specialists within industry does not produce barriers. In the organization charts the lateral lines are clearly indicated, but it does not follow that departments always inform horizontally as well as vertically. It is important, for this reason, that the job description given to an individual should clearly indicate to him his responsibility to communicate and consult laterally with other people concerned. What is, of course, also most important is to ensure that the three channels of communications from top to bottom, bottom to top and sideways should not be so cluttered up as to block the passage of essential information. The utmost thought and consideration should therefore be given to the amount of detail that needs to be communicated. The golden rule is to cut out detail as much as possible, communicating it only to those who really require it for managerial purposes. Detail and information should be carefully sorted. The great danger is to deluge with detail the higher levels of management, that can make no real use of it, and so provide an alibi for more junior management when they fail to make their own decisions.

Paper passing is the bane of modern business and it flourishes like the green bay tree. Now and again there is a purge, but like cigarette smoking after a heavy tax imposition the impact is short-lived and growth begins again. The purge is, of course, useful but it is not the real answer to reducing the paper passing. Getting rid of paper, which is expensive both in preparation and time spent in reading, begins with the top management. It is the chairmen and managing directors who should be constantly pruning the information papers that they receive. Very often information upon a specific matter is called for at the top. It will go on being supplied until it is made clear that it is no longer required, its purpose having been served long ago. Indeed the people who complain most about the amount of paper they have to read and handle are usually the very people who should stop it flowing. Each level of management should ask of itself the question, 'Do I need this regular return for the purpose of my work or decision-making.' Eliminate all the regular paper to which 'Yes' cannot be the answer and substantial savings arise. Very often regular statistical returns are really inessential but from time to time the information they provide could be necessary for decision-making. In these cases the regularity of returns should be stopped and spot answers provided to questionnaires as and when required. I repeat what I have said earlier and what Professor Parkinson has indicated so admirably in his book on the subject, that the flow of paper unless checked will grow and grow, increasing the work load and the personnel needed to deal with it and adding unnecessarily to costs. The chair that each administrator sits upon is a mighty expensive piece of office equipment, possibly costing anything up to £300 a year before salary costs.

Human engineering means making the most of the energies and capabilities of people on the payroll, keeping the number down to the size required to run the business and eliminating as much paper work as possible. Good communications mean adequate knowledge and information at the right time in the right place and to the right individual or group of individuals. Bad communications are like a man who winks at a woman in the dark: he knows what he is doing but she doesn't.

7 Safety

The 'laissez-faire' ideas of the nineteenth century, centred as they were on self-help and individual responsibility, meant that employers and management were reluctant to devote much effort or expense to the safety of their workers. This attitude gave rise to many of the myths which still plague the industrial safety scene today, such as the concept that safety and high output are somehow contradictory aims and that accidents are always caused by careless workmen.

Indeed it was the State which first recognized the vulnerability of employees and brought in legislation to ameliorate their conditions, often in the teeth of fierce opposition from all concerned in the industry to be covered. There were of course enlightened firms which directed some effort to the goal of safety, either from a sense of moral obligation or a recognition of the efficiency which could result. However, most firms would, and did, react with stunned disbelief to the suggestion that they should possibly have any responsibility for the safety of their employees. Their duties seemed clear in the terms of the contract of employment, and if a person accepted the work and the pay then he also accepted the consequential hazards. Thus accidents were part of the way of life, and debilitating illnesses or deformities caused by the conditions of a particular industry became the accepted feature among people in that locality.

The State's intervention in this field was a crucial factor in

121

obtaining improvements and many Acts of Parliament were passed, dealing with conditions of work in factories, mines, and transport, which laid down minimum standards of safety, maximum hours of work, the limitation of child and female labour and provided for full-time paid State officials to ensure that the legislation was observed. The position of semi- or non-industrial workers was dealt with at a later date, but by the dawn of the twentieth century attention was clearly focused on achieving acceptable minimum standards of safety for all workers.

In a sense, the legislation which achieved so much carried with it the built-in disadvantage of provoking resentment and resistance from the employers and management, who have their attention constantly directed to the minimum requirements of the law. Thus it is true to say that a real appreciation of the importance of safety on humanitarian and efficiency grounds has never gained universal acceptance. The Factory Act is too often regarded as a necessary evil, and the inspector a busybody whose efforts management must strive to foil, or at best against which they must defend themselves. In some industries there is a definite 'them and us' relationship between management and the inspectorate, which often prevents true co-operation developing.

The factory inspectorate would seem to face an impossible task. Its terms of reference embrace the whole field of industrial safety, health and welfare in over 200,000 factories and a similar number of building sites, offices, shops, certain railway premises, docks, warehouses and other institutions. The size of the problem they face is illustrated by the fact that in 1968, 312,430 accidents causing death or absence from work for three or more days were reported, which cost the country an estimated £600 million. To fulfil this enormous task the factory inspectorate musters only 621 inspectors and is provided with an annual budget of just over £2 million. Indeed they are often as many as 40–50 inspectors below strength, and when specialist and administrative staff have been deducted the routine work of inspection devolves upon about 200 or so full-time qualified inspectors. The policy has always been to attract university graduates to the post of factory inspector, but the salary offered is far from attractive. This undermanning must gravely impair the efficiency of the service, and the situation is not improved by the fact that the average penalty for a prosecuted infringement of the Act is around £30 (although the maximum is £300). It has been suggested that this penalty is insufficient and should be reinforced, perhaps by imprisonment, but it is not clear how far the courts would go along this path. In any case the further development of the safety theme should in my view be angled away from legislation, and be incorporated with other techniques as part of the science of good management and human engineering. Indeed not until wise managements recognize the importance of safety at the place of employment as an integral part of efficiency will the requirement for inspectors and enforcement virtually disappear.

Why should we concern ourselves more than our forefathers with the subject of safety and what is the significance of safety to human engineering? First, we do not regard human suffering so lightly as the nineteenth-century entrepreneurs. Secondly, the cost and waste caused by industrial accidents is staggering and simply cannot be tolerated in the continuing economic struggle facing this country. The total number of new claims for injury benefit in 1968 was 937,000, which resulted in the loss of more than 24,000,000 man days. Accidents therefore claimed more time than industrial disputes, a fact which received scarcely any publicity at all, yet burdened the economy with the tremendous bill of £96 million in claims for social security payment alone. The average lost time per accident for a man is twenty-five days and thirty days for a woman. Although there may be an amount of 'swinging the lead', the fact that a man is away from work on average for at least three weeks means a tremendous disruption of output, and unnecessary, wasteful redeployment of resources to counteract this effect. Even more

123

fundamental, the poor safety record in industry helps to engender the 'us and them' attitude and accentuate the workers' distrust of the motives of management.

The apathy towards safety in most of industry results in the misuse of safety officers, where they exist. Indeed there are basically two types of safety officers: the professional performing his life's work, and the man appointed (usually from the shop floor) so that the company can claim to have a safety officer. The latter usually does not possess the experience or training to undertake the vast amount of work expected of him. It has been mooted that standards would be raised by creating a professional status for these officials: an idea which should not be dismissed lightly.

As he is not usually a member of line management the safety officer has a most exacting advisory function. Not only must he inculcate the correct attitudes among the workmen, but he often finds his biggest battles in convincing his management colleagues of his proposals. Yet it is in the development of safety consciousness within the company in both men and management that the real progress will be made. Safety organizations throughout the country are asking for more power for the safety officer, but there is another side to the coin. If the safety officer had authority to demand or instruct there is a danger that he would become the company's 'resident inspector', and his proposals be treated with such open or veiled opposition that he would in fact lose the co-operation which must be the foundation of any progress. His message is surely strong enough as it stands. If he is a well-trained and qualified member of the management team he will be able to demonstrate to his colleagues that a few pounds spent on safety equipment would save hundreds of pounds in lost production time, and incalculable degrees of unnecessary human suffering. The question, therefore, is more one of status than authority, and status depends ultimately on the ability and expertise of the individual. Like respect it must be achieved, it cannot be granted or imposed.

In fact much is being done to improve the standards and training of safety officers, and hence their status. A number of residential and non-residential courses are held regularly by the British Safety Council and other safety organizations, and the Institute of Industrial Safety Officers (with a membership of around 1,800) is continually organizing meetings and discussions. This activity should be reinforced by the right attitude among the men at the top. If it is recognized that top-level decisions are made with safety as an integral item in the deliberations, then the status of the safety officers down the organizational levels will be enhanced. Similarly the safety officer's improved training will enable him to make clear, specific, scientific analyses and recommendations which will command respect. The ill-founded notion that he is a general 'do-gooder' with rather unhelpful, obstructive and woolly ideas will disappear, and his valuable potential contribution will be realized.

One thing is very clear: acceptance of the status quo so far as industrial safety is concerned represents more than just inefficiency, it is industrial sabotage of the first magnitude. There will be no final solutions to this problem, nor any short cuts. The solution of one difficulty only clears the path to the next. The only slogan we can adopt is that 'one avoidable accident is too many'; and I would qualify that immediately by accepting that there is no such thing as an 'unavoidable accident'. I have already discussed the role of safety officers in this struggle, and the enormous task facing them. Their greatest challenge and opportunity lies in demonstrating to management that safety means efficiency.

I have already, in earlier chapters, argued that a good environment at work is vital to efficiency. The safety of man at work is part and parcel of this concept.

With a growing number of safety officers providing increasingly skilled guidance it is part of the task of design and operational engineers to include safety as a fundamental item in their management techniques. It has been established beyond any doubt that safety can, and should, go hand in hand with record breaking productivity increases. When management throughout the industrial scene have really appreciated the truth of this message the improvements in both safety and efficiency will be astounding.

What then should management do? Perhaps the best answer to this question is to ask another. Does senior management spend any real time on this matter at all? By and large the answer must be that it figures low in the priorities. It cannot be said to be ignored, but it does not rank as high as anything which can be seen to have a direct bearing on profit. Yet here is a field that can in fact add considerably to the profit line of a company and at the same time relieve a good deal of human misery. When one reads the annual reports of inspectors, one cannot help but be struck by the number of accidents which by common consent it is agreed should never have happened. 'The human failure' is explained with a half-apologetic shrug of the shoulder. But this is an explanation which should be held as wholly unacceptable. Safety in the place of work is so important from every point of view that it just cannot be left to the display of safety posters.

Only very rigorous discipline and regular safety inspections can obviate the 'human error' and this must of necessity be a well-organized routine. Every accident, large or small, should be investigated thoroughly with a view to identifying causes and eliminating those causes so that it is impossible for another accident to occur again for the same reason. This is easier said than done, I know, but nevertheless the strong effort has to be made. Management down the line should be made to realize that the safety record is one of the factors that senior management take into consideration when judging the efficiency of junior management.

There are very few unforeseeable accidents. In the main, accidents are due simply to lack of thought, lack of consideration, carelessness, a failure to comprehend the consequences of inattention and sometimes deliberate intransigence.

Strong discipline must be exercised, and must be plainly seen to be exercised, upon those responsible for contributing to or causing accidents. This exercise of strong discipline is absolutely essential if the folly of thoughtless people is not to fall as a monstrous burden upon the backs of the innocent. One must never overlook those who lie behind the man at work. When the father of a young family loses his life or is permanently crippled by an accident at work, he is represented only as a statistic in the scheme of things. The terrible weight upon the mother and children plays no part in any statistical report.

Senior management must not simply accept that a serious accident has unfortunately happened, but regard it as their job and responsibility diligently to inquire into and search out the factors that led to the occurrence. Fixing the responsibility is important: very often the incapacitated man is responsible for his own personal tragedy, through a touch of carelessness, but there are other occasions when the injured individual is the victim of other people's carelessness or failure to observe the procedures laid down by management. Identifying the responsibility should be accompanied by a proper degree of disciplinary action.

In all matters of safety and discipline the workers should be involved: there is nothing to beat self-discipline, and Safety Committees composed of management and work-people at all levels are certainly the best way to reduce accidents. Safety at work is largely a matter of good management and close co-operation between work-people and management.

Good management means good communications, and the principles which I have already dealt with apply as much in the field of safety as elsewhere. Where safety officers are appointed it is important to ensure that they are taught to communicate properly. Having all the knowledge at one's own fingertips is extremely useful for oneself, but not very useful

127

to others unless it can be communicated properly. The message of safety has to be conveyed succinctly and simply. The problem of communication is very often ignored and in many places no solution is sought for because it is not even recognized as a problem. The whole question of adequate and efficient communication was high-lighted in the Chief Inspector of Factories Report for 1967. I can do no better than quote his exact words:

> One of the major obstacles to the effectiveness of a safety programme is the perennial problem of achieving adequate methods of communication within the works. However forthright the policy of management, however clear the chain of responsibility, it is essential to ensure that work-people are sufficiently involved, and not only understand why rules and procedures for safe working exist, but are kept constantly aware of the relevance of these rules to their own particular jobs. In practice, successful communications usually depend upon the ability of the foreman or supervisor to talk to the workers in his section. It is there-fore encouraging to note a gradual spread of safety contact schemes, which basically require the foreman, at regular intervals, to discuss with each of his men in turn a parti-cular safety topic, on which he has been carefully briefed.*

The appointment of safety officers, or area safety advisers when the firm is too small to employ a safety officer of its own, has proved to be a great boon, but the appointment of such personnel must not be allowed to be a reason for the non-interest of the foreman or supervisor. The new industrial Train-ing Boards, now covering over a half of the working population, are providing safety courses in their schemes, and there is undoubtedly a growing acceptance that good industrial train-ing must include safe working in all its aspects. This growing realization and the considerable increase in safety activity will in due course bring about the desirable result of reducing the

* Annual Report, Chief Inspector of Factories, Cmnd. 3745 (H.M.S.O., 1967).

injury rate. But it is all too painfully slow and will continue to be painfully slow until each separate management realizes the necessity of doing something dynamic about safety in its own bailiwick.

The trade union movement too has a major part to play in all this. National, regional and local safety councils abound in which the trade unions at national and area level play their part. But here is an area in which the vital role is played by the local officials and shop stewards, and they should be encouraged to play an active part in accident prevention.

All this is a vital part of human engineering: if we spoil metal in a process, then regrettable though it is the scrap heap claims it and every effort is made to improve the engineering to avoid a repetition. Good human engineering could prevent much human material being scrapped or damaged, with all the attendant misery and hardship.

8   Delegation

Man is an animal of great curiosity, who loves to delve into the whys and the wherefores, the hows and the howevers. It is this curiosity and interest which marks him off from the rest of the animal kingdom and has provided the driving force behind the tremendous material progress that mankind has made over the last 3,000 years. Curiosity is an essential ingredient of human nature, but like so many good things in life it can become a vice rather than a virtue if it is allowed to range unchecked. In our everyday life we all know to our cost that the dividing line between the good neighbour and the busybody is hard to define and frequently impossible to explain. This, of course, is largely because busybodying, like beauty, is in the eye of the beholder: we want neighbours not nosyness and to make matters worse we insist on defining the terms ourselves. We like people to take an interest in us and if they don't we call them 'stuck up' or stand-offish, but we do not like 'folk taking too much on themselves' as they say up North. We want to be accepted as part of the community but we want to live our own lives. This is a feeling that starts early: one of the inevitable cries from the heart of all youngsters from the age of five upwards is 'stop treating me like a child'. Some parents find this an impossible request even when their children are adults. The danger in industry is that this attitude may apply to fellow workers and subordinates.

130

Unfortunately our toleration does not necessarily improve as we get older. The likely response to an over-zealous interest in our affairs is the invitation to 'mind your own business', sometimes slightly modified in deference either to politeness or fear of a punch on the nose to 'You mind your business and I'll mind mine'. This is a commonplace enough phrase which normally and naturally provokes an emotional rather than a rational response, yet oddly enough it expresses one of the fundamental maxims of good management practice. We are too inclined to think in our day and age that the problems of management are somehow intellectually so difficult that they require the whole apparatus of scientific research and investigation, backed by the latest panacea the computer, before they can be tackled. The truth is that most of the diseases of industry are only too simple to analyse: it is the acceptance of the diagnosis and the willingness to swallow the medicine which is so difficult to find.

One of the major weaknesses of management is failure to mind one's own business: to do one's own job properly and not to interfere in other people's. Most people accept this as a truism and like all truisms they then proceed to ignore it. For what is a truism but a once widely accepted truth that has been repeated so often that it no longer makes any impact on us? It goes in at one ear and out of the other without meeting any resistance on the way. Because of this, while few will argue with the basis of the proposition, even fewer will pause long enough to think of its implications and validity to their own particular circumstances, and only the select few will try to put it into action. These select few are likely to be the good managers and leaders of men.

The art of doing one's own job and nobody else's is one which calls for considerable self-control and skill and is a ripe field for human engineering. The conventional approach to modern management often seems to pay scant attention to this basic human problem in the frantic, wearisome (but no doubt highly

131

profitable) search for the deeper truths of management science. Many organizational structures which have been carefully worked out to meet every conceivable need of the firm turn out in practice to be disastrous failures because of a complete lack of appreciation of the basic need to make sure everyone is able and willing to follow the homely injunction 'You mind your business and I'll mind mine'.

The organizational chart is only as meaningful as the way it is operated. A good example of that is the modern football team. The programme is really the organizational chart of where each individual will play in the team, but once the game begins we find the full backs taking on the role of the wingers, the centre forward playing in the centre half position and so on. In this case the organization chart has become meaningless and contributes nothing to the effectiveness of the business in hand. But each member of the team must nevertheless know precisely what his role is and it is his success or otherwise in minding his own business which has a bearing on the performance of the team—not his position on the organizational chart.

I am, of course, begging the question a little. There is little doubt that most people would agree that both at home and at work we should all concentrate on our own affairs. That we should all, in the widest sense of the phrase, 'mind our own business', but the battles begin to rage on what are rightly 'my' affairs and what are not. In our social life this state of affairs has to be accepted but its possible effects are softened by society's conventions of good manners and the lubricant of civilized behaviour. It is only when conventions collapse or the intrusion is so great as to shatter the glass of politeness that trouble arrives which has to be settled by some form of combat, physical or legal, depending on the emotions involved and the size of the combatants' bank balances.

When, however, we are dealing with matters that do not just concern ourselves, but the organization for which we work, then these differences of view as to what is 'my own business' have to be settled in a different way. Decisions on what has to be done are taken by variants of two apparently opposed forms of organization. The first of these is the hierarchical system, in which power stems from individuals in accordance with their respective places in the pecking order and in which orders from above have to be accepted without question. So what is 'my business' will be decided by my superior and may well change from day to day or even from minute to minute. The best example of this is, of course, an army. The very nature of the battle is such that the speed and authority of decision-taking is of the first importance: no one would dream of taking a vote at the height of battle to see whether the troops wanted to advance or retreat, not just because any attempt to settle strategy and tactics by a democratic vote is likely to result in a most unsuccessful campaign but because it would not be physically possible.

The democratic organization is at the opposite end of the scale from the hierarchical and is the theoretical basis for our trade unions and co-operatives where decisions are taken according to the will of the majority. The very nature of the democratic process is time consuming and inhibits rapid action, but we value it for its other virtues. Here, what is 'my own business' can be decided by the votes of the members of the particular group. This works only so long as people in the minority, even though they may strongly disagree with them, are willing to accept the views of the majority, and this can be a hard lesson to remember and accept.

Because 'right' decisions have to be based on full information which not everyone can have, not surprisingly even the most democratic institutions today have a strong hierarchical tendency. The paradox is solved in a simple way. The decision as to who should head the hierarchy is taken democratically but thereafter the leaders are left to decide everybody else's duties and places in the organization. This is particularly true of the Mother of Parliaments, which is accepted as our most democratic institution, although one which while it has been one of our most popular, has not been one of our most successful exports.

The leaders of all our political parties are elected by their supporters but once elected they have full power to share out all the jobs going, whether they be Ministries or merely 'Shadows'. The power of the party leader to make these appointments in any way he wants is limited solely by his political judgment as to what he can get away with and not by any democratic mechanism. An indication of how sweeping is this power is given by the Prime Minister's right to change his mind quickly. Take, for example, the way that Clem Attlee decided overnight that Hugh Dalton would make a better Chancellor than Foreign Secretary and that despite his wishes Ernie Bevin should be given the job of tackling the cold war; or the now notorious July Purge of Macmillan Ministries in 1963.

In industry and commerce we get, as we would expect in a free country, the whole spectrum of organizational patterns and all of them, whether consciously or not, are aimed at deciding for every employee what is his or her business and making sure that it is properly minded. Although all types of organization are found in the industrial world, the leaning is towards the autocratic, with orders and instructions being handed down from on high. But as no one and no institution can legislate for all eventualities (not even Queen's Regulations) people at various levels of the hierarchy have to be given discretionary powers. These powers are not exercised in the individual's own right but on behalf of his superiors, who delegate some of their authority to him. The decision on the powers or work to be delegated and the way in which this delegation should be carried out has been a topic of increasing interest to students of management in recent years, and much has been written on the Art of Delegation to make it appear that it is more complicated than minding one's own business and not somebody else's.

134

Every great leader, in whatever field—the army, politics, industry and the Church—has to learn the art of minding his own business if he is to survive either intellectually or physically. Some have learned the hard way; others have had the idea put to them and have grasped it thankfully. History is salted with many delightful stories of the support and council great men have had from their wives, their children and their mistresses, but for some reason the parents-in-law of great men seldom merit a mention. There is however one shining exception: Jethro, the father-in-law of Moses, who over 3,000 years ago gave his son-in-law some priceless advice.

All through the long, hot, arid day, from soon after daybreak until the stars were high in the sky, Moses had sat in the desert listening to some of the hundreds of people in his charge who wished to see him, to talk to him, to seek his advice or maybe his decision on the conduct of affairs for which he was ultimately responsible to God. As each new face came before him he had to consider a new problem, judge the validity of the story that was being put to him, weigh up the opposing arguments, make a decision and send each petitioner away with detailed instructions as to what must be done. All the time his father-in-law sat silently by, watching the way in which Moses carried out his task. When the long day ended Jethro decided that it was time his son-in-law was on the receiving end of some advice for a change, so taking advantage of the time-honoured privilege of parents-in-law to rush in where angels fear to tread, he suggested to Moses that he did not know how to mind his own business. 'If you carry on like this, my lad,' he said, 'you will fall flat on your face. You cannot hope to see all the people who would like your advice and if you persist in trying to do so in this way then you will crack up either physically or mentally. What good do you think you are doing? Although you are working hard you are wasting most of your time on relatively trivial matters which others are quite capable of dealing with. Then you find you have no time left to think about

135

by chance and not by choice and would not enable him to use all his time sensibly on work which only he could do. This is often what happens to modern managers. They tackle the work to hand, whether or not it could be delegated, and they 'delegate' that for which they have no time, rather than that which could equally well be done by someone else. Having delegated the wrong things they naturally get bad results, which fortifies them in the belief that they cannot delegate as much as they would like because their subordinates are not up to their jobs!

Lower down the line, where the pressures are not so intense, such failure to delegate does a company a grave disservice by preventing more junior members of the management team getting their feet wet in decision-taking. It prevents their learning the basic business of management. We all know examples of what can happen when a manager who is a notorious non-delegator suddenly dies or leaves the firm. The whole structure can collapse overnight. No one knows what to do or how to do it. It is fatal in business to have only one mainspring: if delegation were not right from every other aspect the need to train future managers is a strong enough reason in itself for making sure that delegation is carried out efficiently and systematically.

All delegation must be carried out under proper control and with a full realization of what it involves. Opinions will differ as to what this is, but it seems to me there are three main elements in delegation, which, although they merge into each other, are worth considering separately. These elements are judgment, trust and control.

First let us take judgment, that elusive quality which is so hard to define but which is pure gold to any enterprise, big or small, which is blessed with it in its management. Judgment is needed in the art of delegation in deciding what should be delegated and to whom it should be delegated. In a two-man business these questions normally solve themselves. Either the man faced with the task does it himself or, if he feels he either lacks the time or is not capable, then he asks his partner to do it. When the enterprise gets larger these problems are among the most complex that modern management has to face. This is not hard to understand. The delegation of authority means by definition that someone else is being authorized to act as though he was the firm. The decisions he makes are the firm's decisions and more senior management may have to face the consequences, particularly if they are bad decisions. The branch manager of a store may have been delegated authority to decide who shall be his local suppliers of perishable goods. If he has this authority and he chooses badly then all the odium of being a supplier of poor quality foodstuffs will attach to the company and not the branch manager himself. To the housewife he is the company, and if she is sold poor goods you can be quite sure that the word will soon get around that this firm, not just the branch, is a supplier of poor quality goods. The housewife takes that image with her and discusses it with her friends and neighbours over the tea cups and, in no time at all, that firm has a problem. It is no answer simply not to allow branch managers any local initiative, because a good branch manager by careful purchasing locally could have the opposite effect and could get the company a tip-top reputation for quality and freshness of products.

In practice, of course, a good company can overcome this particular problem in a number of ways: by having approved lists of potential suppliers, or random quality testing by headquarters, or a first-class complaints procedure. The point I am making is that it is vital that every company should work out carefully and in detail how the element of delegation in decision-taking can be optimized to free senior management for policy-making while at the same time maintaining reasonable safeguards for the company's reputation. The appropriate organizational pattern has then to be evolved.

The larger the organization the greater the tendency and

indeed the necessity to have more levels of decision-taking, each level being authorized by a policy decision of the parent board to take decisions up to a certain limit, which is usually expressed in financial terms. The greatest care, however, has to be taken to ensure that there are no more levels of authority than are actually needed. With the passage of time Parkinson's Law insidiously comes into force and decision-making levels sprout like briar in a rose patch. It is then that the pruning knife has to be used with freedom and skill. Judging which growth needs cutting hard back and which just a gentle trimming is a job calling for 'green fingers'.

Careful judgment is required to get just the right number of levels. Too many will turn the management structure into a series of post offices with each man in the hierarchy busily engaged in making destructive comments on his subordinates' work before passing it up the chain of command. This is the negation of the management function as it is work-creating rather than decision-taking. Management should be eliminating work, not adding to it with innumerable memoranda and comments.

On the other hand, if there are too few levels of authority this may place too much weight on a few senior managers, cluttering them up with relatively trivial problems to the inevitable detriment of the major decisions.

To ensure the efficient administration of any business, from that of the local fish fryer to the international combine, once the various levels of authority have been correctly established it is essential that no manager should ever do the job of a subordinate. This is a real temptation at all levels, but unless it is resisted the chain of command will weaken at that point. Personal initiatives become stifled and the management effectiveness of the personnel involved weakened. It is the prime task of management to concentrate their time on those tasks that others cannot do. Managers are paid for making the difficult decisions, not for taking off their coats to do the work properly belonging to subordinates. Which, of course, brings us quite naturally to the second element of trust.

It is no use expecting someone to delegate responsibility or power unless he can do it with confidence. There must be implicit trust in the ability of the individual to whom authority has been delegated, and this can only be a certain trust if the selection and promotion procedures and management development have been properly carried out. Even so there is ever present the danger of over-promotion and here the responsibility lies not with the individual who has been over-promoted but by the higher management level that made the appointment. Their judgment was wrong and over-promotion will happen from time to time. This is a most difficult situation but one that must be faced. Where the inability to perform is because of over-promotion then management has the responsibility of providing for the individual concerned a sideways move and ensuring further training before, if possible, beginning the upward move up the promotion ladder again. It would be grossly unfair if the individual himself were made to bear the brunt of what in fact has been a misjudgment on the part of senior management. We cannot expect all our geese to be swans but management, having made a misjudgment by over-promotion, must not pretend that the error does not exist and ignore it in the hope that it will somehow solve itself. This can be a very expensive 'non-action' on the part of the firm. A series of decisions badly taken, or not taken at all, can cost the firm far more than if the man had been paid to stay at home. It is also essential for a change in the management to be made at the level at which the inability has shown itself for reasons of morale, otherwise junior management will see that inefficiency is tolerated and senior management will have to exercise a close supervision which ought not to be necessary, and which is a waste of their time.

Where men fail to accept and carry out the responsibility delegated to them through sheer incompetence or through a

141

falling off of performance as a result of failing to apply themselves properly to their work, then management must, of course, exercise discipline. Delegated work not carried out efficiently can be disastrous, not only to company results but, even more important, to morale. The higher an individual climbs in the hierarchy the more he has to be trusted to work on his own initiative and the more vulnerable he becomes. He should not aspire to high office unless he is prepared to take the growing vulnerability of his position. It was said of Sir Walter Raleigh that on a window of a winding staircase at Windsor where the first Elizabeth used to pass he wrote with his diamond ring: 'Fain would I rise, but yet I fear to fall.' The Queen is reported to have written underneath: 'If thy heart fail thee, climb not at all.' True or false the philosophy is about right; in modern jargon I suppose it would be: 'The bigger they are the harder they fall.' Trust is a very important element in the art of delegation, both for those who trust and for those in whom trust is reposed. I can only re-emphasize that the key to this is selection, training and development, subjects of such importance that I devote my next two chapters to them.

The third element is control. This is essential to ensure that delegated duties at all levels are being effectively carried out. It can only be exercised effectively by giving all management very clear objectives that they are expected to achieve and at the same time limits of authority which are properly understood and accepted. It is amazing how many managers do not have a clear idea of their own responsibility.

Objectives must not only be defined with great clarity but they should be agreed objectives: the manager must know what his objectives are and must fully accept that they are feasible. There is no point in setting objectives for management if these objectives are beyond the capacity, the scope or possibilities of the people concerned. Objectives should therefore be agreed and changed in accordance with varying business pressures.

Then the limits of authority have to be set out clearly. This calls for detailed job definition. When the limits of authority have been very clearly defined management must be made to keep within those limits. Failure to exercise authority up to the limit is just as dangerous in business as over-exercise of authority beyond the limit, and both must be checked. If job descriptions are carefully written then there should be no grounds for management to claim any blurring of responsibility, which is the curse of large organizations.

Statistics provide one very effective means of control and no business can operate without them. The great danger, however, to senior management especially, is of sinking in a morass of figures. It is important to identify the statistical keypoints for each level of management and use these as the signposts for further action. All statistics should serve a specific purpose of management control and guidance.

Delegation, properly conceived and applied, will do much to prevent duplication of effort, but more than that it will bring order to the definition of individual responsibility through all the stages of management. In a large concern there will be very many more management levels than in the average-sized business, but the principles of delegation apply equally to both.

One weakness of otherwise good delegation arises when it results in the failure of individuals to see that the part represents the whole. Delegation must not be seen as the negation of teamwork, and senior management must ensure that the groups of managers exercising authority at different levels combine together to provide the team approach to the general objectives of the business. Time to think, time to discuss are all essentials for top management, and delegation of authority should be such that time to think and consider future action is available to all who in one way or another carry the demanding burden of managerial responsibility.

Half the coronaries and ulcers within the business community

143

are due to failure to delegate and the inability of individuals to realize that while they are important to their business they are not indispensable.

Failure to delegate from the top produces frustration and has an unsettling effect on those below that is inimical to a company's welfare. Perhaps much the worst result is that managerial initiative is inhibited. There are too many 'Ask the Boss' people in management, and too few who make up their minds on the problem and act. The real test of management is decision-taking, not memo-writing, and those who make the grade in management are those who get on with making decisions when they are needed. It is no use making the 'right' decision a week too late. Stafford Cripps used to say that any decision is better than no decision. After all, the very act of not deciding is in fact a decision. There are still too many managers who dilly-dally and are incapable of making up their minds on even the simpler issues. These men are a brake upon progress. Very often they are the product of a not-too-well-managed business, where the art of delegation has not been practised or, if it has, not thoroughly enough.

Failure to delegate leads to gossipy discussions, often long protracted, with not very effective or clear-cut decisions at the end. A clear-cut line of command, no matter how long, where each level of management is clear about its authority and power, produces the right decisions with speed and proficiency and provides an air of confident management which does much for morale throughout the whole work force.

I ought perhaps to include in this chapter a famous but possibly apocryphal anecdote about Winston Churchill. The story goes that Churchill received a long, closely reasoned report from one of his subordinates, concluding with a list of four or five possible alternative courses of action which he proceeded to put in a series of hypothetical questions. Churchill read the document and returned it to the author, with this note pencilled across the top: 'Answer your own bloody questions.'

Delegation needs to take account of eventualities and provide for necessary changing of plans. Rigidity simply has to be avoided. The story of the Schleiffen Plan is one classic example of undue rigidity in an organization. The Schleiffen Plan for the invasion of France through Belgium, which was put into operation in 1914, was prepared by Schleiffen many years before, and in fact, when it was put into operation, Schleiffen himself was dead. However, the German military commanders adhered strictly to the plan as it had been drawn up (despite the fact that some time after he had prepared it, Schleiffen himself had rejected it as unworkable).

A. J. P. Taylor, in fact, has argued that the outbreak of hostilities in the First World War was due largely to the strict planning and time-tables which the military commanders of each country had prepared, and which, once they were put into operation, were irrevocable. The minute the order to mobilize was given, the plans took charge of the men and all initiative was lost.

At the eleventh hour, the Kaiser told Von Moltke, the German Commander, to move against Russia rather than against France. Von Moltke argued with his Sovereign, not that such a move would be undesirable, but that the detailed plans drawn up in previous years made it impossible, and that the only response to Russian mobilization was to move first against France. Surely this is an extraordinary and tragic example of an organization taking charge of the people in it, rather than vice versa.

In a rapidly changing technological society plans need to change much more rapidly than ever we were used to a mere twenty years ago. Provided the delegated authority is clear and accountability applied at each level of authority then changes in planning can be assimilated quite quickly.

Finally, to return to a previous example, there is no doubt

that Jethro knew something about management. But his lessons that responsibilities must be shared in a manageable way, and that each manager should limit his decisions to those which only he can and must take, still have to be learned by many managers in industry today.

9 Education for Management

It will be as well, I think, if I begin this chapter by considering the subject of education for industry in its broad historical context. With history, it is generally difficult to know when to start: but as in so much else in the case of education for industry the Industrial Revolution gives a clear starting point. Industry, in the current sense of the word, could hardly be said to have existed before the eighteenth century. Indeed, it seems that the very word acquired its present meaning then.

Its first clear use to mean 'that part of society concerned with the production of goods' is found, significantly enough, in the great textbook of Industrial Revolution economics, Adam Smith's *Inquiry into the Nature and Causes of the Wealth of Nations*, first published in 1776.

Interestingly enough, much the same is true of the word 'Education'. Its meaning as 'the systematic instruction given in preparation for the work of life' dates from the early nineteenth century; and the restriction of its meaning to that part which is cultural and broadening is first found in John Stuart Mill's *On Representative Government*, published in 1860. And this too is significant, because Mill was also an economist, though one much less harsh and uncompromising than Adam Smith, one deeply concerned with culture, social justice and education.

So we have our first sight of the interweaving of industry

and education, through the texture of the language itself, and the concern of men for the right organizing of society.

The Industrial Revolution, starting in this country, has had a more significant and widespread effect on mankind in general than any other series of events of which we have record. The systematic mechanization of production, the division and specialization of work, and its organization on this basis, the concentration of people in towns, and the whole idea of innovation and material improvement which goes forward and continues, has changed the lives of men far more than any conventional political revolution. It has made them richer, it has changed their culture more, and it has spread its effects more widely than the French or Russian or Chinese Revolutions.

In fact, one might almost say that the only lasting effect that political revolutions can achieve is to release a people to get on with the job of industrialization.

And all this started in England, two hundred years ago, give or take a few decades. This was when modern history started. When we underwent the Industrial Revolution there was no previous experience to guide us, no other industrialized country to provide capital or assistance. This explains, to some extent, the mistakes that were made and the needless pain inflicted. But, taking it all in all, it is a matter for pride, if we can avoid its companion, complacency, that Britain gave to the world this great vision of the possibilities of freedom from poverty, of freedom from the grosser forms of manual labour, and of ever-increasing material prosperity. To adapt the words of a statesman of the time, we saved ourselves by our exertions, and the world by our example.

We did this with no great natural resources, except coal. Our resources were then the people of this country, with their energy, their discipline and their inventive genius. The position is no different now: it was not coal that made us rich then, nor will natural gas now. And, indeed, if the truth is told, it never will be any different. It is always people on whom it all depends.

148

As was said by Macaulay (in a speech in favour of restricting the work of children to ten hours a day):

Nature meant Egypt and Sicily to be the gardens of the world. They once were so. Is it anything in the earth or in the air that makes Scotland more prosperous than Egypt, that makes Holland more prosperous than Sicily? No; it was the Scotsman who made Scotland; it was the Dutchman who made Holland. Look at North America. The emigrants generally carried out with them no more than a pittance; but they carried out the English heart and head and arm; and the English heart and head and arm turned the wilderness into cornfield and orchard, and the huge trees of the primeval forest into cities and fleets.

The mention of human resources, of course, is where education comes in. Consider the history of industrial change following its first triumph in England. Other countries followed in our path, and did so determinedly and deliberately. We tend to think that formal education had little to do with the Industrial Revolution, and indeed in the case of our own experience, being the first, it could hardly be otherwise. We had to invent the technology before it could be taught. Although great inventions, great technical advances were made, they were not based, in general, on an organized body of applied science. They were, in fact, very much home-made. Education only of narrow scope was needed by the situation: and even this was made still narrower by short-sighted, selfish and cowardly views. The iron-masters and mill-owners wanted operatives who could read, clerks who could write and book-keepers who could add and subtract. That was all.

And when I suggest that they wanted their workers to read only, not write, I do not exaggerate. The latest historian of the Industrial Revolution* tells of the dominant figure of orthodox

* E. Thompson, *The Making of the English Working Class* (Gollancz, 1963).

Wesleyanism between 1810 and 1850; one Jabez Bunting, of whom he writes:

> When, in his ministry at Sheffield in 1808, his eye fell upon children in Sunday School being taught to write, his indignation knew no bounds. Here was 'an awful abuse of the Sabbath' ... Bunting was in the forefront of a movement which succeeded, very largely, in extirpating this insidious 'violation' of the Lord's Day until the 1840s.

The historian adds:

> It is only fair to note that the Established Church and other Nonconformist sects (then the Methodists) also forbade the teaching of writing on Sundays.

I need only mention child labour and the name of Lord Shaftesbury to recall why teaching on Sunday was of crucial importance to the children of the working class.

Things went differently abroad. Our rivals imitated us deliberately and carefully. The superior power and wealth of Britain was clear enough to them, and they were keen to get their share. They tried many ways: they would bribe skilled men to come and teach them; and laws were passed in England forbidding the emigration of many types of skill. But basically the mechanism was obvious enough, if you come to think about it. They were not going to sit down and go through the whole process all over; the machines had already been invented, and the technologies were already there, being used. The 'brain drain' is certainly not new.

So they first found out all about it; and then, second, set up institutions so that the knowledge was widely, systematically and swiftly spread. They were not going to sit back and see what happened: the statesmen were too worried about power, and others were too keen to get rich, to do that.

So they wanted some systematic way of bringing about this

transformation. And those who knew of it, also knew perfectly well that it could be taught — after all, they themselves had been taught it. It is no surprise, therefore, to find that by the middle of the nineteenth century the countries of the continent of Europe had fully-grown systems of technical education. The home-brewed, suck-it-and-see stage was already past: indeed, for them had never existed.

But it was different in Britain. This stage was all that was known. People had learned their craft in the factory, not in the technical college. This meant that it was difficult for them to see that it could be taught. It is very hard to believe that what one has absorbed through one's skin, so to say, during a lifetime of experience, can be written down in a book and taught to young lads at school. It is a very deeply rooted feeling. The books always seem to miss out the richness, the subtlety, the emotional colour. There is the feeling of envy: 'I learnt it the hard way, why shouldn't he?'

And there is always the view that the old way is tried and safe: with it we know where we are. If we look round now we can still see it.

Think of management education. This has been going on in America for forty years: it has only in these last few years started in this country, and industry has given millions of pounds to support the two Business Schools at London and Manchester.

But many managers still will not believe in it. One can still hear that managers are born, not made. Well, the good scientist is born, the good teacher is born; but are we to pull down the laboratories in schools, or turn our training colleges into hotels?

As a result of all this, indeed partly as a result of our first triumphant success, technical education in this country started out fifty years behind its foreign equivalents. It is probable that this country's lagging behind others in economic progress, of which we are all so conscious now, started over a hundred years ago with cowardly views on education.

151

The broad pattern I have described can be seen very clearly here, in the Development Areas. Coal and iron, steam-ships and railways, formed the irresistible combination which made the Victorian British Empire and Pax Britannica. The north-east, for example, was built on the fruits of the genius of George Stephenson and the hard work of the Geordies. But change is of the essence of the revolution that they made, and change was too long delayed on Tyneside. The ultimate cause of the hunger marches in the 'thirties was a lack of mental energy which left the north-east stranded technologically, and with it mass unemployment, deep-seated poverty and a burning resentment against society. Ellen Wilkinson, then M.P. for Jarrow, wrote graphically of these events.*

The effects of economic depression and stagnation are only too well known. They are more far-reaching than unemployment, though this is a terrible thing, spreading poverty in widening circles and taking away dignity from men. They induce a general feeling of skimping, of meanness. Plant is not replaced, buildings are not maintained. Industry says it cannot afford to take safety measures, or to deal with its effluents, liquid, solid or gaseous. Management refuses to spend money, to take risks, even though spending money and taking risks might be the best cure for the situation.

Education is a good example of this type of short-term view: it is always among the first things to suffer when the state of the economy demands cuts, and yet education has so much to do with economic progress.

A further effect of depression is the migration of the better-educated, more dynamic young people. They do not move only for jobs and money: they move for a brighter atmosphere and for a more confident, more buoyant, more dynamic environment. It need hardly be said that this may start out as an effect of stagnation: but it very soon becomes a cause. So the area concerned does not just suffer from poverty but from dereliction,

* See Ellen Wilkinson, *The Town That Was Murdered* (Gollancz, 1939).

an ageing population, and a general greyness. A drabness that takes the heart out of living.

Now I have gone into this depressing subject at some length to recall that economic stagnation has effects, indirect but certain, on the quality of life. I am conscious that as a politician turned industrialist, in dealing with education for industry, I am in danger of giving the impression that I regard education as the servant of industry, and that everything should be sacrificed to increasing the Gross National Product. It is surprisingly easy to confuse the standard of living, which the Central Statistical Office measures, with the quality of life, which it does not; and it is also easy to forget that production is for people, and that people need other things than just the products of their industry.

I am aware that education is not only for industry. It is part of human engineering. It is for people. It is for life. Indeed, only one-third of the working population is employed in manufacturing, and although most people will be working at one stage or another, many of them, particularly women, will work in industry for only a few years. But, for all that, the health of industry is closely connected with the quality of life, and is of abiding interest to those whose concern is the well-being of the rising generation.

In the relations between education and industry, the mental energies of everyone working in the field of education should be directed so as to ensure the economic health of this country.

We have seen how we dropped tragically behind foreign countries in the second stage of industrial development: that stage when a national education system was required to produce technicians and specialist technologists. But we have not stood still. We now have a system which is a mixture of institutions run by national and local government, industry and private enterprise. It produces for industry innumerable specialists, from fitters and pattern-makers to chartered accountants and chartered surveyors.

153

Even now, the number of specialisms and specialists increases every year, and there is a certain problem in constantly adding to educational facilities to cope with this. We are all familiar with the new trade of the computer programmer: fifteen years ago it had not been invented. In the last year or so it has divided, and large businesses and enterprises using computers now use what are called 'systems programmers' on the one hand, and 'applications programmers' on the other. Soon, I have no doubt, we will look to the educational organization to train them.

Industry today requires a whole variety of experts such as engineers to specialize in quality control, operational researchers and many others. Indeed, every industry needs a substantial number of specialists in every field to ensure efficient management. To start with, training within industry can develop and is in fact developing these specialisms, but eventually and sooner rather than later industry will need the technical colleges and universities to provide the courses for them.

However, we shall have drawn only one lesson from history if we think the world is going to continue changing in the same old way. Other types of change have already started to come about. These are more fundamental than increasing specialisms, more difficult to appreciate, more difficult to cope with, but at the same time more truly rewarding.

First let me try to describe them, and then discuss the changes they might mean for education for industry.

The rate of change in the specialisms is now greater than it has ever been. This is obvious enough in engineering and science: but consider this in a less expected field. Law is as solid a profession as you could wish to find: the lawyers will not change unless they have to. And indeed I am not aware that the Inns of Court ever run refresher courses for barristers. But I am sure that they would be well advised to do so. New legislation alone would be reason enough; and there is more and more of this. So much so that the House of Commons even talks of reforming its procedure to relieve the pressure.

154

Consider then the opposite end of the scale: the semi-skilled men on a car assembly line. The job is semi-skilled and repetitive, but the car being assembled changes every year in major ways, and in minor ways more frequently. Or, looking through the other end of the telescope, how many people will work on a car assembly line all their lives? If a lad leaves school at fifteen he has fifty working years in front of him. How many assembly lines were there in 1917, fifty years ago, at Dagenham? Or at Cowley? Or in Coventry? Looking forward, it will not be long before old-style assembly lines are fully automated. And who would care to bet that we will still be using petrol engines for individual transportation by the end of the century? The traditional heavy industries and the textile industry have shed many thousands of workers in the past twenty years. There is more substantial shedding still to be done in coal, steel, railways, docks and ship building, all intensive male employment industries. The change in the tempo of the kind of employment is rapidly increasing. Many thousands of men are now doing jobs that will be non-existent in ten to twenty years time.

Take the coal industry, for example. Twenty years ago there were over 700,000 men in the pits, now there are little over 300,000, and by 1975 perhaps there will be only 160,000. A good many people in that period up to 1975 will have retired or died. Even so, these figures mean that well over 100,000 have gone or will be going into completely different industries. And of those who remain precious few will be doing the same job that they started out with. In the last five years, excluding the training given to recruits, thousands of people in coal, including supervisors, instructors, craftsmen and members of power-loading teams, have had to be re-trained to meet the rapid technological changes. Twenty years ago 98 per cent of all coal was won with pick and shovel. Now the figure is less than 8 per cent. The machines have taken over and this means that not only the actual coal-getter's job is totally different, but those of planners and managers, craftsmen and engineers,

155

even that of the Chairman of the Board, have all changed too.

The experience of the coal industry is no different from that of the rest of British industry, except as to size. And this is not a once-for-all change: in fact, the pace of change is quickening. This holds quite generally: no one is exempt. The telephone and the typewriter in the past, the photocopier and the dictating machine in the present, and the data link in the future, all alter office work radically. The computer will assuredly revolutionize every kind of job: not just those of the clerks, but the managers and the designers. In the last few years teaching has felt the influence of change, with the language laboratory and programmed learning.

Now, for society to be able to deal with all this change we need more than re-training facilities and refresher courses. It is extremely difficult for someone who has been rigidly taught a particular skill to learn another one. A man who has sweated through five years of articles to become a chartered accountant, who has had the principles of auditing drummed into him, will find it very difficult to learn operational research techniques. If the facilities are laid on for him, he may eventually get with it, but at what expense, what effort? This is not all: he will resist the new techniques, and understandably, when their introduction means at best a time of re-training and re-orientation about as pleasant as having a tooth pulled. The same holds for all of us: if we have been educated in a narrow specialism, learning another one after maybe twenty or thirty years is an uprooting. Too much intellectual and emotional capital has been spent on inflexible assets. So we must teach people in such a way that they are able to learn.

This may sound strange and paradoxical, but after all we do it to a limited extent even now. Teaching people to read is the first great step. And all the basic skills are to some extent flexible. Everyone knows that addition and subtraction work, whether you are adding apples to apples or tons of coal to tons of coal. We could go rather further than we have in the past. We can all calculate in pounds, shillings and pence—or at least well enough to be getting on with, but I guess, though, that the understanding of the calculation is pretty mechanical. And in the past the primary objective in mathematics tended to be drumming into pupils a mechanical knowledge of the systems of units handed down to us by our ancestors. There was the little verse:

> George the Third
> Said with a smile
> Seventeen sixty
> Yards to a mile

—which sums up pretty well a thoroughly barren teaching, both of history and mathematics. But even without metric and decimal systems we hear of new methods of teaching arithmetic, which give not just an ability to manipulate a particular system of units but an understanding of all such systems.

The change I recommend is an immense one: and I quite accept that we are not able to put it into practice immediately. Let me describe some other changes in the world around us that alter what industry wants from education.

The greater pace of change leads to an increase in the scale on which things are done. Sometimes this is quite simply seen: nowadays, rather than build a row of houses we find ourselves having to build a new town. This is a major difference in scale and gives rise to unexpected problems. When things change slowly, bit by bit, we can see what is happening much more easily. One mistake is not disastrous, and we can learn from it. If you add one house to a town, you do not really need to understand how towns work, you need to understand only how houses work. But it is different if you have to build a whole town. It is no accident that an old country market town is generally a more pleasant place to live than Stevenage or

Newton Aycliffe, for all the modernity of the latter. We are learning, but it is a painful and expensive process.

Now the answer in this case is already under way. If we are to plan towns we need town planners and, indeed, in place of the old borough engineer we find the new town planner. Sometimes it is no more than a change of name: but there are training courses for town planners, and it can be taught quite quickly.

The expert must take a broader view. This does not apply only to high fliers, like accountants and engineers. Apprenticeship schemes need to be radically changed so that the craftsmen can cope with change without having to start again from scratch. Machine operators need to have some training in such things as machine maintenance and running repairs, formerly the prerogative of the craftsman.

The increase of scale I have spoken of is made still more serious by other technical changes. In a report published recently, a team from the British Chemical Industry which had visited America told of a chemical plant built in 1963 which was being mothballed because a plant three times the size was being built, which required only the same number of men to run it. In this country the Central Electricity Generating Board has over 200 power stations; and just 20 of the ones it is now building could supply the whole country. When planning is on this sort of scale, mistakes become much more costly.

Life is becoming much more complex. Consider the services an ordinary house now needs. Two hundred years ago, there was running water, with luck. The Victorians added gas and sewage. Since then we have added electricity and telephone. Television is sometimes piped in, and the district is well rid of the aerials. With major new building projects, there is district heating. Offices need teleprinter and data links.

In the past it was tolerable to dig up the road every time one of these services was added: now this is becoming ludicrous. But to organize it all in advance needs thought and planning, and involves bringing together many interests and many specialist technologies.

This bringing together of experts leads to another need for a new type of man, also with breadth of mind but of a different kind. Industry needs technologists capable of appreciating that there is a wider view than that of their own technology, and capable of working with others towards a common objective.

But the common objective is hardly ever in terms of any particular technology. For example, the ideal car to a thermo-dynamics man might be the one with the highest efficiency. Un-fortunately for the narrow thermodynamics man but luckily for the rest of us, the common objective set to the design team will probably be minimum cost within a certain specification of performance and comfort.

So another aspect of the need for more than narrow tech-nical expertise is the need for men who can control teams of experts, who can determine the true objectives, and who can express these objectives in the language of the experts.

The techniques described so far have been the type that manifest themselves in concrete objects, like machines and houses. But there are others which manifest themselves in abstract systems. The computer people have a word for this: the machines of one sort or another that they make or use they call 'hardware'; while the standard programmes, or sets of instructions, that make the hardware usable they call 'soft-ware'. Now one of the most significant differences between the modern world and what went before is in the software of society. Accounting techniques give one of the oldest examples; industry and commerce could not function without them.

There have been great advances in this field recently, and it is only with such advances that we can hope to handle the complexity of the modern world. Its development is not acci-dental. At the start of the story everything was on a small scale: individuals could handle it without control from above; the economics taught was that of competition and laissez-faire and

159

the education system needed was one which produced specialists. But now the scale of things has increased and individuals cannot cope alone: the firms grow larger; the economics become that of planning and the so-called mixed economy; cost-benefit techniques and the like are developed; and we ask the education system to provide people capable of taking an overall view.

How are we to do this? It will have to be a big change in the end. It will not be sufficient just to give our undergraduate engineers an occasional lecture on Human Relations in Industry, for example. In the case of engineers the answer might lie in saying that we are trying to produce managers: so we must teach them the principles of management in addition to enabling them to obtain specialist qualifications. It so happens that in the last twenty years or so the theory of management has developed far enough for it to make sense to talk of teaching it.

To a large extent it is up to the universities, especially the technical ones, to ensure that industry is not only provided with a large number of highly qualified specialists, but men and women who have the capacity to manage and in particular to manage people properly. Our educational system must develop people with breadth of sympathy and with the capacity to learn. This is in line with the traditional ambitions of educationalists to teach people how to think, not what to think. In the past, the requirements of industry often obstructed this ambition but now, if we understand our own needs correctly, this is no longer so.

Research can be fruitfully used in education, as in industry, and without it any advances will be sporadic and unproven. But there is not enough research into education. In 1959, out of every thousand pounds spent on education, one shilling and tenpence was spent on educational research. Nearly ten years later the figure per thousand pounds reached five shillings, so there is some improvement. But even five shillings is a nineteenth-century figure.

In advocating increased research I am not suggesting a crude conception of the purpose of education based on the measurement of I.Q., forgetting about artistic ability and the understanding of people. The purpose of educational research is not to maximize the number of qualified cost accountants or of passes in 'O' level maths. It means simply getting intelligent people to spend their time thinking about how to educate better, giving them the chance to try their ideas in practice, and finding out which ideas work.

This breadth and flexibility, which in my view industry needs at every level, is, it seems to me, far more in tune with the idea of true education, education for life, than the former call for more highly trained specialists. F. R. Leavis has said that a truly humane education is one which produced 'that conscious and intelligent incompleteness which carried with it the principle of growth'. He was, of course, referring to a somewhat different incompleteness from the one I have in mind, but not so different as might seem at first sight.

All these things involve more than an increase in industrial efficiency: they involve the development of people as human beings to understand issues wider than their own specialism, to work together with others, to continue formal learning even though at the top of their particular tree. I believe this may be truly called 'conscious and intelligent incompleteness which carried with it the principle of growth'.

A society able to push the human genius deeper into the unknown is rich indeed. Despite the logical methods taught in the universities, new mystery and magic are being injected into the lives of quite ordinary people. A new dimension is being awarded to our imagination, a dimension which could not have emerged in anything but an industrial society. We now have at our disposal the power to control and direct nature. We are uniquely placed to create and mould an environment in which human potential can be realized to the full. The human approach should always be at the front of our minds. Technology

L

and industry must serve people, enlarge their lives, raise their standards. Those directing them must remember always their responsibility to people wherever they are in the world.

A world of peace cannot be built upon a large section of humanity living in poverty and deprived of real living. Sciences must be utilized to enlarge human happiness based on the family. These are all opportunities that industrial society has created, and we must never allow these opportunities to slip away by neglecting the basis from which they were so dearly won. We must try to spread the message into the schools that provide the universities with students and into the society into which they will emerge when they have graduated.

Perhaps the most exacting of all the jobs that management has to do is to pick out what is new; to signpost the new way forward; to innovate. So it is with the management of education. Yet throughout our national life, the ghosts of out-moded ideas continue to stalk. I hope that our schools, colleges and universities will not allow themselves to become one of these haunted houses. So much else is: the nervous timidity of some government leadership; the sluggish way in which we sometimes grasp new inventions; and the technological limp we have developed. But so much is fine in Britain —the finest in the world: the robust common sense of our people; the zest and verve of which we are capable. We are a nation uniquely experienced in the rhythm of industrial life. Our human potential is unrivalled and far from fully exploited. Neither North Sea gas, nor nuclear power, will propel the next in-dustrial advance for Britain. Our only asset is our people and it is on our people we must depend. The educational system could easily provide the springboard for this advance. This is why the way in which education is managed is so vital to us all.

10 Career Planning

As companies grow in size, either by merger or individual growth, the problem of providing adequately for management succession becomes increasingly difficult. But the succession must be provided if continuity of adequate and efficient management is to be available for the years ahead. Indeed it is a solemn duty of today's management to provide for tomorrow, and tomorrow's management will have to be that whit sharper than today's if the business is to make progress or indeed to survive. Businesses today are being taken over at an accelerated pace, largely because existing management has failed to make the most of the assets and as a result find themselves at the mercy of a take-over bid. Management, if it is to be the bidder and not the recipient of a bid, needs therefore to be constantly on its toes in an endeavour to produce even better management, as with the advancing years the competition stiffens and rationalization in one way or another is forced upon them.

Fortunately management, like many other disciplines, is an art or science made up of skills which can be taught. It is the process of developing these skills to meet the future requirements of senior management that is the subject of this chapter.

Career planning is one more 'must' for present-day management. Many large companies have already embarked upon career planning and have notched up some considerable success. But so far this occurs in only a small part of British industry, while every firm, large or small, ought to be playing its part in career planning to the advantage of the economy as a whole. Buying management from others does not add to the sum total of managerial expertise, but merely adds to the burdens of those who have trained and planned at considerable expense. The natural movement of younger management from one firm to another is of course necessary to provide the cross-fertilization which is so obviously advantageous to industry generally. But if all companies both large and small were to provide adequate managerial training then the sum total of managerial skill and competence would be greatly increased and the impact upon the national economy would be considerable and quickly noticeable.

Career planning within a company gives not only the guidance and training needed to make the individual more effective in his present job but enables him to prepare himself for the highest level of responsibility of which he is capable. The existence in a company of an effective scheme of career planning and development is an assurance to junior management that opportunities of promotion will be offered in the future that are appropriate to their talents and efforts. This in itself brings a return to the company in stability and reduced turnover of junior staff.

The future prosperity of a company is governed by two main factors: first, the wise investment of capital, and, second, the ability and personal qualities of the people to whom one commits one's money. Both are important, but if anything the emphasis is perhaps rather more on the latter: if top management fails to make plans to ensure that an undertaking has the men and the women it needs, properly related by categories, ages and skills to its objectives as a whole, the future of the company will be as insecure as if its cash flow and capital structure were to fall into disrepair.

The problem of ensuring the succession is not new. The business man of the nineteenth century had never heard of management development and career planning but he practised it just the same. He produced sons. Having done this he prepared them for future management by 'putting them through the mill'. Many a Lancashire family today owe their riches and prosperity to the fact that their predecessors were 'put through the mill'. It was these businesses that flourished. Where later generations were not trained in this way the businesses failed. From this failure of third-generation management came the descriptive Lancashire saying, 'Clogs to clogs in three generations.'

Management training today is not of course so simple. Business is now too involved and complicated for any but the most exceptional and outstanding to 'go through the mill' and come out on top. Life is not long enough to master all the intricacies. Instead young men will need to be selected quite early as prospective senior management and their progress planned by job rotation and promotion so that they are deliberately and progressively provided with the kind of experience that will equip them for the part that they will be required to play.

Increasingly intense competition demands, year by year, more efficient management with better control over costs, so that junior management who aspire to senior positions must be thoroughly trained and ready to acquire a wide variety of experience. Their ability will need to be thoroughly tested in different circumstances, and regular assessments of their performance collected and recorded.

The aim of management development or career planning is to ensure the succession; to ensure that when one manager leaves, another man is ready, not only to replace him but to better his performance. The very process of assessing managerial ability and planning managers' experience, brings with it many useful by-products. If your assessment of a man's performance is to mean anything, you must have a benchmark by which to measure it. When you tell a manager what the benchmark is, you often discover that he previously had a quite false idea of what really was expected of him. He may prove to have been

165

complacent about a low level of performance; more often he is found to have allocated to his work a totally different order of priorities from those which his superiors would have selected. When a manager knows exactly what is expected of him, his energies can be more appropriately channelled.

To this extent, almost every organization has discovered that the introduction of a management appraisal scheme has given new impetus to the improvement of management performance. This is so much so that it is currently fashionable to claim such an improvement as the main aim of a management development system. I myself regard such a distinction as difficult to quantify and hence dangerous. So many factors affect the results of an enterprise that the extent to which sheer managerial skill contributes can only be measured over a period of years. Management appraisal schemes, linked to management by objectives, are still in their infancy in this country, and if the supposed benefits do not materialize quickly, the whole idea could be discredited. I prefer to regard these benefits as a useful by-product to the main aim of management development, which is to provide for the succession.

Providing for the succession is, as I have said, a complex affair in modern industry. A succession policy has to reconcile two conflicting trends. The first trend is that as managements become more scientific more and more areas are coming necessarily into the realm of the specialist. Human engineering itself, the foremost task of any manager, now has to be administered not only by line managers but by a host of personnel specialists. At the same time, we can no longer afford to produce top managers who are ignorant of entire aspects of their organization. A production man who has never in his life worked on the marketing side and appreciated its problems is unlikely to make a first-class managing director of a company in a highly competitive industry. Thus one is searching all the time for the perfect all-rounder while making it ever more difficult for him to get the necessary experience. The provision for this experience therefore needs to be planned, although it often seems to go against the short-term interests of the company. Taking an effective line manager away from the works for two years to put him in a back room with some planners is not usually popular either with the man (for, not long ago, such a move would be regarded as one step short of the sack) or with his superiors (who have to install a replacement and break him in). One has to admit also that the experiment can often be unsuccessful, but the attempt has to be made if we are to avoid breeding a generation of blinkered specialists.

This and other problems only come to light after one has started asking questions about the succession. Who is going to be the General Manager of the Production Division when Smith retires in two years' time? At one time, Brown looked like being the obvious contender, but we have had growing doubts as to his ability to stand up to the pressures of a difficult human relations problem; he is probably best suited to a policy-making job. Jones has the gift of bringing the best out of his men by rolling up his shirt sleeves and pitching into the job alongside them; but he gets lost among the paperwork and he never seems to know whether he is making a profit or not. Robinson is one of the modern school, well educated and with an apparent grasp of broad management issues; but he has only managed a small works up to now and he needs a thorough testing before we dare expose him to this job. We have two years to decide: not long to find out whether our doubts about Brown are justified; whether the provision of a first-class management accountant would enable Jones to do the job; and whether there is any more to Robinson than the ability to give a good impression. Suppose, however, that Smith drops dead tomorrow. One has to make an instant decision. One appoints Brown, only to find that labour costs start rising; or Jones, to be driven to distraction by the difficulty of extracting from him the necessary management information; or Robinson, to discover that you have simply over-promoted him.

167

In management development, as in other forms of business planning, the earlier one starts the better. Medium- and long-term forecasts are bound to be more or less wide of the mark but a modern business cannot survive without them. Unless one has some tentative ideas both about the likely size and shape of the business in ten years' time, and about the men who are likely to be managing it, one is striking out blindly into the dark.

Ideally, with efficient career planning there should always be two or three people at any given time from which to make a choice for promotion at a high level. There is bound to be natural wastage and career planning must allow for some men who are trained, and in training, to move out to other firms. Senior management ought never to be in the position of finding themselves without real options when a promotion at the top has to be made. The purpose of management development is to ensure that staff are given the right experience and training to fit them for the jobs in the business now and in the future; that the most suitable people are selected for posts; and that the performance of staff in post is improved. From the point of view of the staff themselves it is important that their abilities should be used to the full. They need to be stretched in every job they do and they need to be in each job long enough for their work and results to be properly assessed.

This means making an early start on selection, and while there will be those who question this by suggesting that early selection will create an elite, I am afraid that the answer must be that it is inevitable. So long as the opportunity is thrown wide open to those who aspire to senior management and consider themselves, after training, capable of performing all the functions of senior management there can be no quibble. Equality of opportunity is essential to ensure that there is no possibility of overlooking first-class managerial raw material. To start some form of later selection, say at forty years of age, is to leave it far too late to provide the experience and impart the knowledge that is required. Men should be in senior posts by their forties, giving time for say ten to fifteen years in really top management. This is long enough in a very senior post before retirement: the hard work and long hours (no forty-hour week for top management) are exhausting if rewarding. The tasks and responsibilities of leadership wring a man out like a wet cloth, putting a definite limit to energy and sparkle.

If we are thinking of ten to fifteen years on the top management rungs, then we should be selecting in the late 'twenties. The first necessity is to identify the jobs that will have to be filled, together with the timing of the vacancies based upon likely occupancy of the post. This estimate of requirement needs to take account of probable changes in the size and structure of the organization; and of changes in the nature of jobs, the consequences, for example, of the shift to capital intensive units; and of the need for managers to be good businessmen as well as professionally qualified men, capable of making use of modern techniques and aids to management such as computers and operational research.

The system of management development must provide for a constant up-dating of staff requirements to keep up with the changing pattern of the business organization. There will need to be a system for a full flow of information in order to assess the performance and potential of individuals so that they can acquire in substantive posts the experience that they need to develop their potential. This will also enable formal training to be given them at the appropriate stages. The whole object of the exercise must be to prepare the individual step by step for the highest responsibility of which he is capable.

A regular, probably annual, review must be designed to measure a man's performance against the objectives or tasks he undertook, to help him to improve where necessary, and to obtain a better view of his potential in order to identify his needs by way of training and experience in other fields. It should also provide for the individual's own comments on his

169

performance, and on his hopes and inclinations. From this review, and the man's own comments, valuable data can be gradually accumulated, pointing directly to his strengths and weaknesses so that his training requirement is effectively identified and satisfied. Training cannot always take place inside the business, and the best use must be made of the external training facilities. The business schools, universities, polytechnics and colleges, mounting such courses as the Diploma in Management Studies, will be essential elements in the scheme of training if potential top managers are to be kept abreast of all the new sophisticated techniques, both in the professional fields and in the field of business management.

One should not overlook for some people the advantages of foreign visits (with specific remits) and secondment to other undertakings. Broadening of the outlook is essential if career planning is to mean anything at all. Management should always be looking for the man who can lift his eyes above his narrow field and see the breadth of the business as a whole. At every level of management this ability of a man to see the business as a whole while handling the affairs at his own level is vital. These are the qualities that one is always seeking in the rising generations.

If the material is right, then adequate development (costly though it may be) will make of that material the high standard of management which large areas of the business world so desperately lack today.

In a large organization it is quite impossible for the top management to be aware of all the talent lying within the company. It must, therefore, be somebody's job to discover those with management potential. This is obviously a job for the personnel department, and may require the appointment of a management development officer. Whatever system is used, however, it must be one that prevents people being overlooked and provides for more than one judgment upon the individual concerned.

It is impossible to lay down a blue-print for career planning; one can only point out some general principles. The detailed system to be installed will depend entirely on the circumstances of the particular organization. What is very clear, however, is that all companies, big or small, expanding or contracting, must build up management development and career planning, or in the years to come the shortage of really first-rate management will hit the country's economy hard, and the company neglecting career planning even harder.

Each year thousands of young men and women are recruited into business and commerce. The newly developing industries are competing with the old and today the young men and women entering the threshold of life have no lack of choice. As a country, however, we are a very long way from realizing the tremendous potential represented by the human resources now being recruited into industry. This is because career planning is practised over such a small area. I do not take the view that managers or leaders are born and not made. It is true that some people have a natural ability to lead which brings them to the top in any situation, but there are so many people of good quality managerial material who are 'born to bloom unseen', and who if developed in the right way and at the right time could have succeeded as top management. It is perhaps the prevalent belief that the qualities of leadership and management are inherited gifts and that is the reason why so few managements today seek out the men who could absorb and benefit from management teaching and training.

The initial selection of people for career planning for top management, it goes without saying, is of supreme importance. The following qualities in the potential senior manager appear to me to be fundamental: integrity and intelligence, an ambition to succeed and willingness to accept responsibility, the ability to exercise judgment and to work as a member of a team. Given these qualities the process of training can be entered into with confidence.

171

Essentially in modern business organization the art of being in and playing a full part in the team must be exercised to the full, until in turn leadership of the team falls to one of the members. Team management provides strengths where there could be individual weaknesses. Good management leadership must be competent in planning, in initiating actions both short term and long term; in problem solving; in keeping communications open right down the line, and not only functioning effectively but being plainly seen to do so. Efficient leadership is never static; what was suitable for yesterday is not good enough for today, and by tomorrow problems for management will be different again. There can, therefore, be no clear pattern of development for leadership.

The aim of management development should be the development of an individual's skills and aptitudes in relation to the particular needs of the industry. Indeed leadership itself is more a relationship between the leader and the situation than just a pattern of particular characteristics possessed by an individual. It consists of a series of relationships between the leader and his followers, the leader and the organization, and with it all the leader and the political and social environment.

This being so, and because these relationships are bound to change through the years, management has to look for people who will be able in the years that lie ahead of them to carry out the new managerial tasks that a changing society and changing world economy is sure to bring. The leaders of tomorrow being trained now must have flexible minds and thinking to recognize changes quickly and adapt accordingly. Leadership in the future is bound to be more difficult than it was and than it now is because of the very speed of change. But this need not daunt the ambitious aspirant for leadership. Nature has an amazing way of conditioning people and their minds for change, provided always that the mind is receptive and not cast in a firm and static mould.

Management training must provide for the development of

the potentialities of individuals and must not try to turn out the same product by setting common objectives for all those whose careers are being planned. The development of individual personalities is tremendously important: different leaders with different qualities and personalities can be equally effective in their own ways. It is personality and character which are the valuable ingredients in the individual make-up of the leader and must be given full play and never confined. This is indeed the only way in which the variety of leadership resources will be available to meet the fairly unpredictable managerial requirements of the future.

In the greater number of larger business organizations being created by merger and growth the demand for leadership at many levels will intensify. Every promising recruit will not materialize as top management quality, but there are very many rungs in the management ladder of large firms and if present-day management recruits well and trains well, then proper selection and development will bring the aspirant to the rung appropriate to his natural abilities, his educational qualification and training.

If the task of career planning is done with care the individual himself will know when he has been stretched to his limit and will be content with his rung on the ladder even though it is not the top one. It is necessary that career planning should enable men to develop their potentialities to the greatest extent in the particular role that they can best fill. Leadership at any and every level is a very necessary requirement in modern business and the judgment of present-day management in career development is to ensure that men are not stretched beyond their capability. Over-promotion, as I have already said, is culpable negligence, unfair to the individual, unfair to his colleagues and disastrous to the business. This is why it is important that the scheme of development for providing the management of the future must ensure that the individual himself is actively associated with his own training and functional programme. The

M

173

individual cannot be poured like a jelly into a shape that is pre-designed for him. He needs to be adequately consulted and an active participant in the decisions about his own development. This will help him to make the best use of the opportunities that are being offered to him. A rigid programme of training, in which individuals are manipulated like puppets on a string, is the negation of true management development and the best way of destroying the personal initiative which it is so essential to preserve and encourage. The development must be one of growth so that the maturing process takes place easily and smoothly. Industry must provide the condition for growth: the climate in which the human plant can grow in to what the individual is capable of becoming.

As I have indicated earlier, there is no blueprint for career planning: there are, however, principles, some of which I have tried to indicate here. What is very clear is the need for sound management training, suited to the needs of each industry, to provide for the succession at all levels.

11 Conclusion

In recent years there has been a bold renewal of man's urge to 'have a say' in the things that happen around him. In some instances this has resulted more in 'having a go' than 'having a say'. Unfortunately these cases have been the ones that have attracted the sharp focus of public attention. I certainly do not know why this movement has recurred just now—we must leave future historians to unravel the causes—but it has happened and it is a force to be reckoned with.

There has been a well-established trend over the years for men and women to demand an increasing say in the nation's affairs and in the affairs of their locality, at their place of work, schools and colleges. One form of this has been to demand that the Government should press forward an ever-widening circle of influence and should take upon itself new skills and activities never contemplated before. This is participation through the top deck and involves at most an indirect involvement of people. The most recent and celebrated phenomenon has been the growth of direct participation.

Whilst I have been writing this book I have frequently reflected whether human engineering is the enemy or the friend of participation. I certainly do not feel that there is any danger at all of human engineering being shipwrecked in the face of this resurgence. Human engineering is designed to secure the conditions—industrial, educational and social—in which the potential of human beings can be released to the full. This involves the careful moulding of an educational system to nurture what is most useful and beneficial in each individual and to furnish him or her with an outlook helpful to the orderly advancement of society. It involves as well the painstaking development of good communications, particularly within industry, so that each individual has the information necessary for him to comprehend the part that his work plays in the whole design. On the basis of this knowledge he can play a part in the decision-making process of the factory. Thus the renaissance in social attitudes that I have set out takes—like the Renaissance that drew the Middle Ages to their close—a starting-point from man and his potentialities. Human engineering emphasizes the importance of an informed and educated man—in other words the sort of individual who would make *informed* participation a vital and progressive element. There must be many who have been angered by the senselessness of much that has happened in the name of participation. We need more informed participation and less ignorant anarchy; more constructive involvement and less barbarian destructiveness; more positive help and less random pillage.

I think the easiest way to illustrate what I mean is to take the coal industry as an example. On a coal face in one of Britain's collieries twenty to thirty men are involved in each working shift to man that face, cut the coal mechanically from the seam, load it on to a conveyor and maintain the roof support system. Until quite recently the birth pangs of a new face were very painful indeed. We knew that the ideal procedure would have been to train the men for the novel geological and mechanical circumstances of the newly opened-out face and create a situation in which the men are involved in the tactical decisions of the way the face is worked and the levels of output to be achieved. But for generation after generation the wage payment system in the industry destroyed the opportunity of implementing these wise principles. Traditionally piecework was regarded as the only wages system that could induce men to work in cramped, badly lit, uncomfortable conditions. As a result, the birth of a coal face was accompanied by a chorus of demands and counter-demands over the correct contract or price list that suited the geological and other circumstances. Working out a piecework system that took account mathematically of all the exotic geological variety of Mother Nature was no mean task. This haggling remained a positive barrier to the orderly implementation of proper participation; a major obstacle that had to be removed if men were to take their rightful place in planning the mining operation at the face.

It was therefore essential to get rid of the outmoded piecework system. Luckily the process was helped by the technical changes in the mines which eliminated the shovel at the face and made power loading machines almost universal. So now the speed with which a man worked was not determined by his own effort, but by the speed of the power loading machine alone. Piecework at the coal face has now almost entirely disappeared and will become a memory within the next months.

So now the decks were cleared for the sort of participation I mentioned; that is the involvement of the people concerned in the tactical decisions at their own place of work. We have now carefully drawn up a programme of what the coal industry colloquially calls 'face teach-ins'. Here the entire power loading team is taken off the face for a couple of days, sometimes to the comparatively academic atmosphere of the local technical college. Here the task of coal getting at the new coal face is explained and debated. Finally the men are invited to discuss the coal output objectives for the face. Very often the men themselves will suggest higher objectives than the management first propose.

In this way the first months of the life of a new coal face can be spent in fruitful co-operation between men and management, rather than in civil war. Silverwood Colliery, one of the first experiments, has become a byword in the coal industry for this co-operation. Here was a pit in the tough South Yorkshire coal-field well known for the uneasy relationships between men and management. With the abolition of troublesome piecework, an avenue was created for a more constructive dialogue between the two sides. When teach-ins were organized for the men going on to a brand new face, management cautiously pitched the output objective at a level based upon an earlier more negative attitude. After having had explained to them what the face was capable of producing and what the technical, geological and — most important — human delays were that acted as a brake on output, the men themselves were more than anxious to raise sights higher and show what could be done. As a result high objectives were accepted and the face has consistently achieved those object-ives ever since. Naturally there have been ups and downs, but industrial relationships at Silverwood Colliery have moved off in new directions and things will never be quite the same again.

I have gone into this in some detail because I think it illus-trates precisely the drift of the argument in this book. If we can create the right conditions and atmosphere, identifying and then removing the obstacles then a new era can be opened up. For almost the first time, the men on the face could give the colliery the benefit of their experience and common sense. Their commitment to ambitious output objectives was won simply because they themselves took part in, and very often led, the discussions that made way for the fixing of output objectives. So the right conditions can take the lid off human capabilities and the benefits of this can be boundless. Direct participation, where it is informed and constructive, can be of enormous benefit to the participants and to the country alike.

Indirect participation, through the advancement of Govern-ment influence, has a similarly chequered history. This advance-ment has taken place under Governments of every political complexion — indeed, Labour Governments, oddly enough, have played only a small role in this development. But the same principles apply here as we have discussed above. Intervention must be educated and informed and the framework within which intervention takes place must be correctly engineered.

The indirect participation of people through all the trappings and apparatus of democracy is worth looking at in detail because it is not at all self-evident that the trappings are efficient and the apparatus well oiled. The earlier chapters of this book described the way in which Britain almost alone two hundred years ago was able to turn invention into the instrument of production. This was something quite new, and Hugh Trevor-Roper* put it well when he pointed out that

> The Byzantines invented clockwork, of a kind—and how did they use it? To levitate the emperor in order to dazzle the ambassadors of barbarian Europe. The Chinese invented gunpowder, and what did they do with it? They used it, largely, to amuse themselves with firework displays. The Tibetans discovered turbine movement; but they were satisfied to exploit it for the rotation of prayer-wheels.

The early captains of industry in this country, with the help of a skilled and adaptable work force, were able to do what the Ancients had failed to do: they used invention for the creation of wealth. Now we no longer depend solely upon the captains of industry to propel industrial progress, because the Government has taken upon itself the role of a feudal economic king presiding over his semi-independent and often rebellious feudal barons—the industrial corporations and the unions.

The competence of the Government—the tip of the pyramid of economic feudalism—should be examined in some detail. Men and women are primarily interested in the economic activities of Government. Winston Churchill said in his Romane's lecture in 1930:

> The Nation is not interested in politics, it is interested in economics. It has in the main got the political system it

* *The Rise of Christian Europe* (Thames and Hudson, 1965).

179

wants. What it now asks for is more money, better times, regular employment, expanding comfort and material prosperity.

I have in the past talked about the idea of Great Britain Limited. This amounts to a bundle of propositions which concern the efficient and business-like operation of central government. This is not to say that private industry is every time and everywhere efficient and business-like, but when one looks at the enormous impact of Government on the economic fabric of the country then Government must be the starting-point.

About £33,000,000,000 is spent each year in this country on goods and services of all kinds. Out of this, Government-controlled expenditure amounts to £11,000,000,000 — almost as much as the entire Gross National Product of Sweden and Holland put together. On top of this the Government is responsible, though less directly so, for the expenditure of the nationalized industries and the local authorities.

This growing public sector is not to be deplored because the job we, the public, expect the Government to do has expanded enormously. How have we let this Leviathan grow in our midst? Two hundred years ago the Government was largely a diplomatic agency, an instrument of law and order and the organizer of national defence. Gradually, as the momentum of the Industrial Revolution gathered strength, great swirling social changes produced acute human problems in the new factory towns. The Government then took on the job of setting minimum standards of public hygiene and education.

At a later stage the mounting confidence and militancy of the working classes created by the new factories pressurized the Government into setting about the correction of social and economic inequalities. This period culminated in Lloyd George's reforms just before the First World War. The aftermath of the 1930s led to new and outraged demands that Government should guarantee full employment. And so the

Government machine has over the years crept closer and closer to the economic heartbeat of the nation. The final phase has come in the late 'fifties and 'sixties when growing public unease about our dreary economic performance forced the Government to burrow deeper into economic affairs in terms of regional planning, industrial restructuring, incomes policy and promotion of efficiency.

This trend is not to be deplored. If there is any criticism to make it is that the movement has been too slow rather than too fast. If the Government is to look after one-third of the spending of this country; if it is to embed itself so deeply into our economic life; if it is to become more and more embroiled in the business life of the community—then it must become more business-like itself.

Many businessmen are riled by Government intervention, not because it is done, but because it is done badly.

I think it is useful to ask oneself the question: 'How would a businessman organize the economic management of central government?' First and foremost he would make sure that his Civil Servants, i.e. his chief executives, did the total sum. It is no good cutting costs in one direction only to see new costs sprouting up somewhere else. After all, at the end of the year there is only one bottom line at the end of the balance sheet. Unless there are groups of men looking at the whole gamut of economic life then we shall continue to limp along in a fairly uncoordinated fashion. This is a powerful argument for centralization—not necessarily the centralization of decision-making but certainly the centralization of setting national objectives towards which the whole economy can work. No businessman would smother enterprise by taking unto himself all the tactical decisions that are made, but he would establish a strategic framework within which the enterprise of his officials could work effectively.

We should be looking continuously at the way in which the Government organizes its task. We might very well conclude

181

that considerable economies could be made by combining the job of paying in and paying out. There are 60,000 Civil Servants in the Inland Revenue (pulling in the cash) and another 60,000 in Social Security (handing it out again). To combine the two could clearly be a great saving. It would also avoid the hated Means Test because the Inland Revenue already have much of the information about income and family commitments that the Social Security people need.

The actions of the Civil Service should be judged on cost effectiveness. Mr MacNamara, President of General Motors of America, who became the American Defence Secretary, made the administration of the armed forces of America a highly efficient machine. Even if we may disagree on the use to which it is being put, there is no doubt of the efficiency — of cost effectiveness — based on his industrial experience.

We should also ensure that as much enterprise is shown as possible — a little of the buccaneer spirit is needed amongst our civil servants. After all, it was the inventive genius of the British people in developing the steam engine, the spinning jenny and all the other paraphernalia of the Industrial Revolution that set the world alight. In order to do this it may be necessary to hive-off some of the responsibilities of Government to independent Commissions. Here they would be free of the day-to-day financial control of the Government and they would be at greater liberty to show the enterprise and genius that we have. Commissions to look after dereliction, Health and Energy could have an enormous contribution to make.

Very often Ministers are bogged down by the detailed work of their departments and constituencies. They have no time to take a long view, to do the total sum, to ripen the vision that leadership requires. I see no reason why we should not develop a dual-purpose Cabinet, one in which there are men of wisdom who are free of departmental and constituency matters to ensure that the whole of the Government machine is conducted in a business-like way. We certainly need business-*like* government in the United Kingdom but this certainly does not automatically mean that we should have business *man's* government.

Planning today is piecemeal and fails to have overall purpose. Patching up in one spot creates problems elsewhere. The fire brigade is running hither and thither to little fires because there has been no overall plan of fire prevention. Since the war, under successive governments, there has been no firm grip upon the economy. The result has been economic disaster—stop, go, stop, go, involving two spasms of devaluation.

A private business managed this way would have gone bankrupt. Here we are over twenty years since the end of the war having to brace ourselves for what is described as 'painful sacrifice'. Too much departmentalization, a failure to devise sound business methods of administration and a lack of the 'total sum' approach have, among other failures, led us to this sorry pass. And make no mistake, unless this nettle is grasped we shall only build up for the next bout of economic illness.

Neither a family, a business nor a country can live beyond its means, and where there is no effective control the bank balance is expended before anybody is aware of it.

It is not only the cash balance that is needed in running a country, the people themselves are the most valuable asset of the nation. A business-like approach would clearly want to look at the human assets at its disposal, how they should be trained, given experience and deployed. It would undoubtedly wish to broaden their experience by giving them training in other spheres of life; it would want to make sure that they were at all times fully acquainted with the latest techniques of business management.

In the same Romane's lecture I referred to earlier, Winston Churchill went on to say:

The economic problem for Great Britain and her Empire is urgent, vital and dominant. There exists at the present time no constitutional machinery for dealing with it on its

183

merits, with competent examination and without political bias and antagonisms ... Yet we do most grievously need to find in a reasonably short time a national policy to reinvigorate our economic life and achieve a more rapid progress in the material well-being of the whole people. It might well be that the measures which in the course of several years would vastly improve our economic position actually and relatively, and open broadly to us the high roads of the future, would be extremely unpopular, and that no single party, even if they possessed the secret, would be able to carry their policy in the face of opposition by the others. In fact it would probably be safe to say that nothing that is popular and likely to gather a large number of votes will do what is wanted and win the prize which all desire.

The defence strategists have put their finger on the problem in an illuminating way. They have dressed up a haggard but vital formula; that commitment should always equal capability. In other words, the weaponry of our armed forces should be appropriate to the treaties and foreign interests that government policy has agreed upon. The machine must be designed for the task it has to accomplish. Governments have now accepted a commitment to become overlords of the whole spectrum of economic activity, but they sadly lack the capability. Unless we introduce this business-like approach at the point of power; at the point where decisions are made; then we shall never pull ourselves out of the slough of economic difficulties.

I wholeheartedly agree with Winston Churchill:

Nevertheless, the task has to be done. Britain is unconquered and will not fail to find a way through her difficulties ... the compass has been damaged. The charts are out of date. The crew have to take it in turns to be Captain ... yet within this vessel there is all the might and fame of the British race and all the treasures of all the people in one-fifth of the globe.

I am for a business-like Britain, and a group of people sitting together could produce a blueprint of government administration which could both give us a sound business approach to our affairs and preserve our cherished parliament and democratic control that would ensure that we do not move into the trap of a corporate state. Britain is great because its people are great, democracy is vital if they are to give of their best in a business-like Britain.

The concept of human engineering is simply the membrane that has held together the fabric of this book. Anyone who has spent time in public affairs would, like me, have been impressed by the quality of people on whom we must rely, and whom we must encourage and guide. Everything that has changed the face of this globe over the last centuries has been the result of human activity.

Human engineering is certainly no agency for confining men and women to a preconceived mould; rather it is to promote the circumstances in which people—making the choice themselves—can realize their potential to the full. This simple principle is as true in the home as it is at work and in the government of the land. Every moral code and every system of ethics which has been devised by man boils down to a group of very simple propositions. Man has a bundle of physical needs: food, shelter and clothing. He has a number of social needs: the yearning for good fellowship and the stimulation of congenial company. Finally he has a constellation of mental needs which drive him to learn about his environment and to nourish the inwardness of his existence—the spiritual side of his nature.

In the past the maddening and often brutal scramble to provide for physical needs has smothered satisfactory human fellowship and orderly mental development. In this book on human engineering I have sought to demonstrate that all three

185

elements are closely bound up together. No family can be a happy family unless parents can create the home environment in which their children develop to the full. The best cannot be given by people at work unless management comprehends the social and mental needs of the individuals in their employ. No government will prosper if it ignores the total needs of the community and fails to accept their advice and participation.